The Heart of Gardening

How to Have a Successful Life Through Sustainable Gardening from a Storyteller's Perspective

REBECCA BAND

CLAY BRIDGES
PRESS

The Heart of Gardening: How to Have a Successful Life Through Sustainable Gardening from a Storyteller's Perspective

Published by Clay Bridges Press in Houston, TX

www.ClayBridgesPress.com

ISBN: 978-1-68488-152-9 (Paperback)
ISBN: 978-1-68488-153-6 (Hardback)
eISBN: 978-1-68488-154-3

Special Sales: Most Clay Bridges titles are available in special quantity discounts. Custom imprinting or excerpting can also be done to fit special needs. Contact Clay Bridges at Info@ClayBridgesPress.com

To my Will, Cheyenne, and Claire. Without you I would have never been able to care and love so deeply.

Thank you to everyone who believed in me, especially when I didn't believe in myself. I hope I can return the same gift to all of you.

Contents

Preface ... vii

The Heart of Gardening ... 1

Getting in Touch with Your Inner Artist ... 11

Designing a Garden ... 24

The Organic Lawn ... 33

Organic Lawn Care ... 44

Healthy Lawn Maintenance ... 55

Raised Bed Vegetable Gardening ... 59

Insects in the Garden ... 67

Food as Medicine ... 77

Beneficial Microbes ... 88

Compost ... 91

Compost Tea ... 96

Earth's Antidepressants ... 102

Water Is the Source of Life ... 107

Drought-Tolerant Gardens 116
Bringing Nature Indoors 120
The Herb Garden 128
The Annual Garden 154
The Perennial Garden 176
The Vegetable Garden 186
Gardening by the Moon Phase 196
Weed Control in Gardens 198
Prepping the Garden 203
The Veggie List 205
The Power of the Rose 238
The Goal of Gardening 244
Epilogue 247

Preface

Gardening in Southeast Texas is continually rewarding. It is therapeutic—a source of healing spiritually, physically, and emotionally. Finding the healing from the connection to the earth's soil, plants, and wild creatures only occurs when you're submerged in nature. The need to write this book came from family, friends, and acquaintances who encouraged me to share my knowledge. I never imagined I would write a book. It wasn't until I left one of the best jobs of my life that the idea of a book would come to fruition. I was asked questions about what I will do with my knowledge. Will I start a YouTube channel or a blog? Both of which I have no desire. I neither need nor want to be so incredibly public with my life. A book seemed to be the most fitting way to share my knowledge. I decided to write an interesting and uplifting guide to gardening in Southeast Texas. It would be something entertaining yet packed full of helpful information about where to start, what plants to choose, diagnosing common issues, and how to solve them organically.

For those who are contemplating whether this book is for you or something to continue reading, I would like to begin with a disclaimer. This is not a book that is in just one category. Rather, it encompasses many categories. My primary intention is to inspire others by sharing my gardening and plant knowledge and how to do it organically, sustainably, and economically. To do this precisely, I will share my personal observations and the way I interpret my findings, which is why there are many personal stories. I could research all day and compile information to represent my experiences, but I have chosen to share my stories because I know them to be completely true. Everything in this book has been tried and proved by me in my own gardens. We all have a story to tell, and this one is mine. It does not make me special; in fact, I hope it makes me relatable. In those respects, this book could be considered a do-it-yourself book and a gardening diary or journal.

I do not consider myself a writer. All my writings outside of secondary education have been poetry and journaling, which I do sparingly. For me to make sense of what is in my head I had to pray and meditate every morning before I began writing—asking God for the right words so people could understand the way I think. My scientific research work for the University of Wyoming's Agriculture Department on suppression of noxious weed seeds in a low-till or no-till system sparked my lifelong curiosity to learn how and why everything works. It also gave me insight into how easily data can be manipulated to show desired results, which is why I apply logic to all things I do. In those respects, this book could be considered a philosophical book.

Most importantly, this book is about the connection of all living things—from the moon and earth to the microbes in our guts and soil—and how we cannot live, survive, or heal without all of them. It is also about allowing yourself the freedom of creativity, using the gifts of the earth to make a positive impact on all life, including people. I've included charts of herbs and vegetables, when to plant, where to plant, and how to use them with recipes I have spent years developing. In that way, this book could be considered a health and wellness or inspirational book. It might be unlike anything you have ever read. That is why I am leaving it up to you, the reader, to determine what category this book fits into.

The Heart of Gardening

My friend gifted me a book for Christmas almost a year before I embarked on my own writing journey. It was *The Artist's Way* by Julia Cameron. What an excellent book to inspire and teach all people how to tap into their creativity! I completed the book and began the process of writing my own book on what I love most about gardening and plants. Two months into writing and for no reason at all, one of the many customers who shopped at my old place of business popped into my head. I thought, *I wish I had gotten her phone number before I left. I think I am healthy enough to finally have a friendship with her.* Almost two weeks later I ran into her at a different darling little nursery. It seemed as though our lives were parallel. We both had quit the jobs we loved, and she had just started writing a book as well. For the last couple of years, it has been her presence that has kept me focused on my end goal.

Then the mom of one of my daughter's friends offered to edit my book, which was another sign that I was headed in the right direction. And one year after beginning this book, the mom of another of my daughter's friends offered to help guide me in marketing the book once it was published. Those were all the signs I needed to know I was on the right path.

Ralph Waldo Emerson's vision of success in his poem "What Is Success?" helped create many of my core values. It was the inspiration I had kept in the back of my mind as my adventure through life as an adult began.

What Is Success?

To laugh often and much;
to win the respect of intelligent people
and the affection of children,
to earn the appreciation of honest critics
and endure the betrayal of false friends;
to appreciate beauty;
to find the beauty in others;
to leave the world a bit better whether by a healthy
child, a garden patch, or a redeemed social condition;
to know that one life has breathed easier
because you have lived.
That is to have succeeded.

My grandmother, Frances Jean Pavlak, wrote down this poem and included it in a letter she sent me when I was just beginning college at the University of Wyoming. Her letters were always so sweet and uplifting, and they included a small drawing every time. The drawings showed me more love than words could express because they were personal and came from the heart. I can remember the impact Emerson's poem had on me the first time I read it. It was the first thing to make sense to me. Money, power, and good looks were not important to me, and I couldn't understand how so many people were governed by those few empty things.

My grandmother wrote the poem on an index card that I hung on my refrigerator at every apartment and every house I lived in for years. I don't remember the exact time I lost it or threw it away, but I do remember it was barely legible and had water marks and rips all over it. The part I miss the most is the handwriting of my grandmother—a lover of life, an artist, and a short story writer. She succeeded, although to how much of her actual potential I am not sure. My fear is that if I have important information and don't share it, I am not living to my full potential either.

In my teen years through my early thirties, laughing often and much was my goal. I sought out happiness. I craved it. I wanted to find happiness and enjoy every given moment. Driving on Wyoming state roads with huge blue skies that go on forever over golden, red, blue, purple, yellow, and silver landscapes. No one was around for miles on end. Birds flying, antelope racing, and deer forcing me to test my brakes as they dashed across the roads. Hiking on trails high in the mountains at elevations most people don't enjoy because the oxygen in the air is limited. Finding an isolated lake made by snow or glacier melt stripping naked out in the open, jumping in the ice-cold water, to feel the rush of life go through me. Smelling the forest floor with its heavenly lush musty fragrance, then stepping into an open field of wildflowers and wild grasses. Being kissed by the sun, smelling the sweet fragrance of grass blooms. Feeling so small and insignificant. Feeling so close to heaven like I was right at home. Finding a secret fishing hole. Scoping out the perfect place to sit and wasting my day in nature, quietly, except for the sound of the plop of the worm on the hook on the clear water. Blup. Christmas tree hunting on cross-country skis or in the middle of the night. Hiking by the light of a full moon, especially in the winter with the shimmering of the snow. The sparkle of icy snow on a sunny day.

My favorite parties to attend or throw were camping parties or drinking in the wilderness with bonfires. My sister's car once lost its tailpipe going down a washboard dirt road on our way to camp out with friends. We retrieved it, and later that night after chasing beer down with whiskey, I turned the tailpipe into a didgeridoo, which left a dark black circle around my mouth for the rest of the camping trip. It was wonderful! One summer, my friends and I enjoyed a full week camping in an old, abandoned gold mining cabin we hiked to. We used the stream from freshly melted snow high on the mountain as our refrigerator. We cooked over a campfire using only a Dutch oven. We caught fish all day long, drank wine all night, played the guitar and harmonica, and slept like logs.

I traveled across the country and around the world finding adventure so exciting it made my heart smile. Sharing the time on the road with adventurous friends who were not afraid of camping off a dirt road, on a beach, accidentally on a Texas rancher's property, right outside Area 51, in the foothills of North Carolina, and eventually on the Appalachian Trail, completely unprepared. I sought laughter, and adventure always brought it.

Attending the University of Wyoming was also a source of joy for me. Many of my professors saw intelligence in me that I did not see in myself. For my senior year, the director of the history department offered me the very best scholarship—the Mary Lou Pence Scholarship—which I did not feel worthy of. The only thing I had to do was apply for it and write a short essay. I wrote the worst essay of my life and still received the scholarship. That is the quantity of potential he saw in me. He believed I would become a lawyer and study water rights law and change the world. It's in my nature to try to sabotage anything good for myself. I was always drawn toward intelligent people. Something about their thought processes and conversations stimulated my brain like no other. And intelligent people were drawn to me. Looking back, I wish I could have trusted the intelligence others saw in me and believed it for myself, but that didn't come naturally until much later in life.

How do you win the respect of intelligent people? That, I'm still not sure of. Perhaps it's willingness to have an open mind, to confidently speak your philosophies or beliefs, to seek knowledge in all areas before forming an opinion, and to be humble. Although I am considered an expert in my field, I don't even know 5 percent of horticulture, and the more I learn, it feels like the less I know. It's just like we know a whopping 5 percent of the universe, 5 percent of bacteria and fungi, 5 percent of our brains, and less than 10 percent of the ocean. Most of what I know is from trial and error, passed down knowledge through friends and family, opinions and research conducted by trustworthy people, and following my instinct with the latter being the most important. Once I was able to view gardening as a whole picture, not just what was right in front of my vision, the process of life began to be clearer.

It has taken me a long time to learn how to be a friend, something that never came naturally to me. I have always been accepting and inclusive of everyone and have intentionally ignored obvious signs of insincerity for the sole purpose of being accepted by the group. Until recently, my desire to be accepted always put me in a vulnerable position. I have been hurt time and time again. I now understand why people intentionally want to hurt others because it makes them feel just a tiny bit of relief from the hurt they are holding tightly to inside. It happens all the time even by good people. I am guilty of it as well.

My innate desire is to see through human faults and straight into the potential of the kindness and love in their hearts and souls. If we as people gave ourselves a chance to heal from whatever fear or hurt we have endured, our true potential and pure love will be exposed. The qualities I look for in friends are the qualities I must be willing to have. Those qualities are the courage to try new things, move away from home, embark on adventures, and find the excitement and joy in life for exactly what it is. They are unconditional love, honesty, and the ability to have different beliefs and opinions while valuing and respecting each other. And finally, it is the comfort to speak freely without judgment.

Appreciating beauty has never been a challenge for me. I am drawn to all things created from the heart. Food made with love and intention has never tasted better. Homemade gifts have more value to me than anything bought at a store. Vegetables grown from the garden have never had more flavor; they don't need spices because they have real flavor all their own. The sweet earthiness and color are special gifts given back to me from my garden. When eating fresh food from the garden, I can feel the minerals and nutrients nurturing me from the inside out. Songs written from the heart, poems, a handwritten letter from a friend, sunrises on the beaches of the Gulf of America, sunsets from the front porch of our house, and the way the crystal hanging from the west-facing window catches the last rays of sun for the day and casts rainbows on our walls. Wildflowers in bloom; burning a fire in the fireplace with the heat, crackle, smell, and the colors of the flames that continuously dance and capture my attention. I just let myself melt into a trance and bask in its warmth. Architecture in the hearts of cities where history meets the future, allowing my mind to wander into the past while marveling in the present. Even as an adult, I still pretend and imagine "what if"—what if I was living here 100 years ago. What would it feel like? What would I look like? What would be the force that drives me? What if I was living in the city today? What would I be doing? Would I walk, drive, or take a train or bus to get places? Who would I meet, and what would be my guiding force?

I find the beauty in others. Everyone has that special gift or light inside of them—their own potential. Seeing the beauty in others is so much easier to do than seeing the beauty in myself. Until I was able to like and then love myself, I was not able to fully do the same for others. It took a lot of work. I used to envy people who seemed to grow up loving themselves, but I have yet to meet anyone who truly has. Looking through photos with my seven-year-old daughter at a presentation in her class, I heard the adult criticisms she was giving herself. "My chin looks too fat. My smile looks too fake," she said. Where does that come from? I thought if I showed her enough support and approval, if I complimented her on the things she is good at, if I didn't say those things about myself, she wouldn't be so critical of herself. It turns out that being kind to and loving yourself is something learned, not something given. There is nothing I can say or do. She has to figure out for herself that she is lovable and needs to be kind with her words about herself. Adults who love themselves appear to have it all figured out and miss so much hurt. At the same time, without the hurt and sorrow, how would we know what true happiness feels like? How would we learn how to find the joy and beauty in all living things?

Having children changed my perspective of how I view myself. I used to not care how I hurt myself by choices I made—not until I had someone in my life who was completely dependent on me. Then I knew my choices affected the health and outcome of the life growing inside me. It also became clear that my choices affected the natural world and society. Prior to pregnancy, I was dependent on synthetic gardening and home-owning practices. I worked at a garden center, and we were taught to be able to offer a solution for all problems. More often than not, the solution was chemically based. Using a water-soluble fertilizer on plants twice a week to make sure they were in constant bloom for consumers to buy was common practice. When I broke out in a rash on my hands after using the product while pregnant, I thought of what kind of potential harm it was doing to the fetus inside me. What kind of potential harm was it doing to the land and water surrounding me? Who drinks that water or eats from the land? Who else and what else was being affected by the consumers' desire to see blooming plants in a garden center?

Gardening has been my therapy—my source of internal, spiritual, mental, and physical health. There is always something new to learn and research. It has given me a sense of accomplishment and has built my self-confidence. It has been the best classroom I have ever been in and the most peaceful sanctuary. And now I want to share my gift with people who want it—a guide to creating your own sanctuary while enhancing your own personal health.

An example of this just happened yesterday and five years ago. When the threat of COVID-19 shut down our whole country, I stayed at home with my girls who were four and seven. I watched the news, and the fear it spread over the entire world was unlike anything I had ever experienced.

Getting in Touch with Your Inner Artist

The first step to creating the space of your own secret garden is to get in touch with the artistic ability God has given you and tap into not just your property's potential but your own potential as well. At birth we are given a destiny chosen by God. I know this to be true because there would be no reason for me to be on earth if it were not true. I was born unresponsive and not breathing. It was considered an emergency, but through the grace of God, I am here. My father told me that before my first breath while the doctor was holding me upside down by my feet, I opened my eyes looked into his, coughed, and cried. He said, "You were supposed to be here on this earth in this life. Either I was supposed to teach you something or you are supposed to teach me something. We have met before in a different life." Of course, throughout my life I have had no doubt in the existence of God and guardian angels.

There have been moments in my life where no explanation can justify how I made it out alive. One such moment happened to me when I was twenty-one years old. I was driving from Jackson Hole to Buffalo, Wyoming, on a wintry night in December. I was driving down the Bighorn Mountains on Ten Sleep Pass in the pitch dark because it was near 11:00 p.m. The wind began to pick up, and before I knew it, I was driving in blizzard-like conditions. Driving at night in blizzard conditions is, to say the least, almost impossible. The reflection on the snow from the headlights was blinding. But I was a seasoned blizzard driver. I'd been driving in these conditions since I was fourteen, and I knew this road like the back of my hand. I had been traveling from Buffalo to Jackson and Jackson to Buffalo since I was sixteen when my parents divorced and my mother moved to Buffalo. However, on this particular night, all the conditions were just right for disaster. As I was descending toward Buffalo from the peak and right before a switchback, I hit a patch of black ice.

My heart jumped from my chest all the way up to my eyes. I may have overcorrected it and then just tried to not go off the cliff on my right side. After three or four complete 360s, I ended with the tail end of my vehicle in a ditch on the side of the road closest to the mountain. I don't know how I didn't fly off the mountain if not by the grace of God. But now I had a new dilemma. I was stuck with only a snowboard to help me get out of the precarious condition I was in. Sitting behind the steering wheel, I lit a cigarette and contemplated my next move. I hadn't seen another driver on the road all night. No one was traveling that late at night on the remote backroads of Wyoming during a blizzard.

I checked my water supply. My vehicle's fuel was almost on empty, but I had winter clothes and shelter. I could make it through the night, but I didn't want to. I bundled up in snowpants, snow boots, jacket, hat, ski goggles, and heavy gloves. I got my snowboard and began digging the snow out from around my tires. After only twenty seconds of digging, I saw lights coming up the mountain road. The car, an Oldsmobile two-wheel drive dark brown-maroon with County 10 plates, stopped on the road. County 10 is Fremont County where the Wind River Indian Reservation is located. Two doors opened, and three men, all Indian, stepped out of the car. The wind stopped, and all was quiet. The driver, wearing a long trench coat and sunglasses (I still don't understand why he was wearing sunglasses at night while driving in a blizzard), approached me and asked if he and his friends could try to push my Jeep Cherokee out of the ditch. In awe and elation I agreed. They barely touched my Jeep while I pressed the gas, and I was out, just like that. I thanked them profusely, offered them a cigarette to which each refused, and they got back in their car and quietly and gently disappeared up the mountain. It felt like a dream. As I drove down the mountain cautiously, because the blizzard began again, I kept asking myself if all that really happened or if it was a miracle.

Were they angels? I believe so. I believe moments and doors open up for us at just the right time. Each of us has a different divine plan mapped out that we must be willing and brave enough to follow. Signs appear, but if you're not looking for them, you won't see them. Leading up to this book, this knowledge really began to reveal itself. In my life, many adults have seen the potential in me. The weak and insecure guides in my life who tried to bring me down to their level were the ones I was inclined to follow because it felt like an easier path. I've always been drawn to people who were hurting because I recognized and felt comfortable in that pain in my own life. I admired the people who were healthy in their soul but never felt I was worthy of their friendship; that is, until I became a mother.

The first gift I recognize God has given us is the gift of love—*the* most important thing in the world. It energizes me, and it is because of that energy that I'm able to accomplish goals. Giving and receiving love is what gives me confidence to be myself. Having love builds and encourages bravery. The first time I was in a reciprocal love relationship was during college. It was because of that love that I was able to take twenty-one credit hours, work a full-time job at the Cathedral Home for Children, and have a part-time job doing research for the Agriculture Department at the University of Wyoming. That was the only year I had straight A's in all my classes. I took the GRE and passed without studying. Life was good, and I was completely happy. But that relationship happened when I was young, and I couldn't see what other people saw in me. I didn't allow myself to be totally myself, and he didn't get a chance to love the real me. We broke up when he moved to Antarctica where he met the love of his life.

When I met my husband, I was just making it day to day.

I found a job as a diesel mechanic, which I loved. And I loved every guy I worked with because they all seemed to have very strong core values. They were hard-working, strong, creative problem-solvers. I showed up to work early every day and left late. Every time I fixed a problem, I felt I had accomplished something I could be proud of.

It was a cold evening in late September when I met my husband. My very first road call was for a driver who was fully loaded and hauling diesel fuel. One of the inside tires on his trailer had blown out. When I saw him for the first time, my heart sped up a bit. He was so cute with his Carhart jacket, piercing blue eyes, dark clean-cut hair, and a trucker hat sitting high on his head. I wanted to talk to him, but more than that, I wanted him to notice me and hopefully fall in love with me.

It was on week three of real official dating that I knew in my heart that Will was the one for me. I felt comfortable and safe to be vulnerable. For the very first time I was completely attracted to his smell, looks, and courage for staying true to his morals and values. He impressed me, and for the first time ever, I heard someone say "the good Lord" in regular conversation. I wanted to have his babies and grow old with him. Being with Will gives me enough energy to do anything and gives me the security to dream and be creative. He also keeps me in check by helping me hold myself accountable for the things I say and do, making me a better person with every passing year.

The second gift I recognize God has given me is the gift of

joy. Even as a child growing up in a family where there was so much chaos and stress, I found joy. Nature was my security, it was my church, and it was a four-dimensional painting where all the senses could be stimulated at the same time. My mother was raised by an alcoholic World War II veteran who handled his feelings with beer and gambling. It's what I remember about him. He would silently wait in his chair facing the clock and TV, acting like he was watching the TV but in truth was watching the minute hand on the clock until it hit twelve o'clock even. With a yawn and a stretch, he would say, "Gal, I guess it's time for a beer," as if he just happened to notice the time. My grandmother also drank a lot. She was lively and a character, always telling stories using accents. She kept eyes off Grandpa by focusing all the attention on herself. Everything she did was creative, artistic, elegant, and classy. She came from a wealthy Irish Catholic family from New York. My mother grew up in a house free of rules. She was a hippie, a nature child. She ran away from Arizona to California to follow Jesus, drugs, and the promise of finding eternal joy at the age of sixteen. My father was raised in a different kind of chaos. His father, also a WWII veteran, died of polio when my father was four, leaving behind my grandmother to raise three children—ages six, four, and two—by herself with no job. She remarried, moved to Arizona, and had two more boys, living off a postal man's honest wages. My dad was always ambitious, participating in everything he could. He played football, was in band, and loved to sing. His dream was to be rich and own horses and a ranch.

My father met my mother at a bar in Arizona. At the time, my mother was married to her first husband who was abusive. My father, whose instinct is to protect, immediately was drawn to her. My mother is tall, thin, and beautiful, a combination of Irish from my grandmother's side and Polish from my grandfather's side. She has olive skin, thick wavy brown hair, one green eye and one brown eye, perfect slightly full lips, and a slender nose. She was the life of every party, always smiling and laughing, drawing attention due to her incredible beauty. My father is handsome, tall, and slender, with thick wavy dark hair, brown eyes, and a brilliant mind. His nose is kind of pronounced, and his upper lip is thin with a full lower lip. He has discipline and drive. He saved all his money from his first job after college to travel around Europe for five months. Before he met my mother, that was his dream. After one month in Europe by himself, he sent her a ticket to come and travel with him. Their love grew on this adventure together, living out of backpacks, exploring, and surviving off $10 a day. Wine, cheese, and bread were their staple meals.

Upon coming back to the states, my parents were married, living in Arizona, and soon expecting my sister. After my older sister was born, they packed up a trailer and headed out to find a place to start their family, a town they would call home forever. After two months on the road, they found Jackson Hole in Wyoming. My father's heart thumped for the mountain town, and the three of them happily lived out of a tent for two months before buying their first trailer. My father opened an accounting practice of his own and grew from there. Two years later, I was born.

The first house where I remember the garden my mother created was when we lived in a log cabin. I was five, and the garden was huge. It was my job to pull weeds. I harvested and ate everything I could right there in the garden. I couldn't help myself. My father grew his business, and my mother grew plants, but only for three months a year. The rest of the year, my parents began to grow apart, and my sister and I grew taller. Divorce is horrible. It breaks so many hearts. In some cases, like this one, it was necessary. I find divorce to be a weak way out of solving problems. But both people have to want to solve problems and grow better. I was still able to find joy, sanity, and security in nature. I can understand people who can find joy even while in a death camp or a societal lockdown. You have to; that is how you survive.

The third gift God gave me is forgiveness. I have the ability to forgive. Unforgiveness is not an issue for me. I forgive those who hurt me almost immediately. It took me about twenty-eight years to learn how to not allow people who hurt me to get too close to my heart and that when it was time to walk away, to walk away. My mom and I have not been in touch since the first birthday of my second child—nine years. Instead of seeing her part that she played, she finds it easier to blame me for her shortcomings in life. Ever since I was a baby, I have been her scapegoat. She struggled to love me, hold me, or be around me because I cried too much. My mother blamed me for my father not loving her. She blamed me for the divorce and his subsequent marriage to my stepmother. My mother didn't understand how healthy relationships work, so any relationship had to have an ulterior dirty motive. She blamed me. I forgive her. I always have and always will. Forgiving her is easy. Forgiving anyone who hurts is easy. They hurt. Hurt is heartbreaking pain that is suffocating. But it's not just the ability to forgive her. I have had to learn to forgive myself because I am human and not perfect just like everyone else.

The fourth gift God gave me is creativity. I am drawn to creative people, art, and God's paintings all over the universe. My perception of the world around me and the education I have are completely different from other people's. That has caused me to hold my tongue because the way I view concepts is not what I have been taught. Following strict guidelines and having rules for every little thing stifles progress to the point that nothing gets done and no changes are made. I dabble in all things art because creativity follows no rules. I love oil painting. The color combinations and smell are so relaxing. I love sewing and making quilts, curtains, and napkins. Feeling fabrics and absorbing the colors and textures are so peaceful. The hum of the sewing machine is calming. I love making jewelry using real stones, shells, pearls, and seed beads, knowing that each piece I create has some sort of meaning and each bead has been touched and loved by me.

There was a time I wrote poetry, but I never felt comfortable enough bearing my soul on paper and sharing it with others through that form of art. I love cooking, combining different flavors and not using recipes or measuring spoons. I love harvesting fresh herbs, vegetables, and flowers from the garden—laying them out in an artful way and implementing them in our meals. I love canning, fermenting, and growing bacteria. The ability to grow life through microorganisms is so exciting to me. Creating art in my garden and waking up to all the colors and life at all times of the year is like walking into a painting I have made.

It is because of this inner creativity that I have *love*, *joy* and the ability to *forgive*. It is incredibly important to dabble in all things creative to see what brings the heart the most tranquility. You cannot create a garden if you do not open your mind up to what creative potential is building up inside of you. A dear friend of mine enjoys cooking, sewing, and decorating her house for parties or just for nesting. She is building her garden around her newly discovered artistic ability in creating the most gorgeous floral bouquets I have ever seen by foraging in her backyard for the material.

Tapping into my inner artist didn't happen overnight. It took baby steps and small habit changes here and there—waking up early, making a cup of coffee, breathing, and writing unrestrained any and all thoughts that popped into my head. Everyone has a special creative gift we were born with as part of our destiny. It takes time and hard work to identify what that special gift is. The easiest thing to do to begin the unwrapping of the inner gift is to set an artist's date with yourself once a week for at least two hours—completely uninterrupted time. An Artist's Date is a special technique I learned from reading the *Artists Way*. That may seem hard to do, especially when raising a family, but it is so incredibly necessary. Not only will you begin to find your inner artist but you will also be nurturing your soul. My two-hour dates with myself give me tranquility and calming of the mind. They allow me to solve problems faster and build my confidence in everything I do. Here are some suggestions to get started with artist dates.

- Deep-clean a room or two in your house. Deep-cleaning a house feels like deep-cleaning and organizing your soul. It involves:
  - Removing every book from the bookshelf and dusting them off
  - Washing the windows and picture frames
  - Dusting and oiling the wooden furniture
  - Washing all the blankets, curtains, and vents
  - Vacuuming, sweeping, and mopping
  - Organizing drawers and cabinets
- Walk through a neighborhood away from where you live.
  - Inner city neighborhoods are a delight.
  - Walk through neighborhoods during the holidays where there are warm decorations.
  - Walk through neighborhoods with very old houses in older parts of the city, perhaps with

gaslights on the front porches and fresh-cut greenery.

  - Transport your mind to a different time when things were simpler yet involved more work and energy from each person to make a feeling of joy apparent.

- Pull weeds from a garden.
  - Listen for the sounds of the wind chimes gently swaying in the wind.
  - Listen to the water from a fountain, creating a tranquil environment.
  - Put fresh mulch on the flower beds, gently snugging it around each plant.
  - Trim off dead foliage and flowers to allow another round of new growth and blooms.
- Take a bath with fresh rose petals, comfrey, essential oil, fresh herbs from the garden, and mineral salts.
  - Play relaxing spa music and drink a glass of wine or hot herbal tea by candlelight.
  - Pamper and take care of your feet by rubbing a stone found at the beach on the bottom of them.
- Make curtains for a room in your house. Picking out the perfect fabric alone is a wonderful

adventure. A quilt store is the best place to find the right material. You don't have to know how to sew in order to make curtains. When all the curtains in my house are complete, I may consider making quilts for each room. I love the hum of the sewing machine, a good romantic movie on TV, and zoning out to good feelings.

- Make a brand-new dish. Find the best recipe or make perogies from scratch. Make souffles or pumpkin pie from a real pumpkin. Make every part of the meal from the crust to the sauce. Then sit with your favorite people and enjoy every mouthful of love and hard work.
- Make something special whether it's jewelry, napkins, a painting, or just a hand-painted card with all the special things you love about a person written inside. Putting into writing kind words for loved ones fills my heart with joy and builds my own self-esteem.
- Design and build a new garden. This is not only exercise, but it is a sign of hope that there will be a future. It's also beautiful scenery that all my neighbors, friends, and family get to see, experience, and believe in as well.

Designing a Garden

When I look at my property or if I am doing a consultation for gardens belonging to other people, the first thing I do is ask:

- What brings a smile to my heart?
- What feeling do I want to experience when I come home?
- What do I want my environment to provide for me?

What brings me joy? Colors, fragrances, and textures bring me joy. I love walking around my gardens focusing on each plant and what special qualities they possess. For example, petunias clean pollution better than any other plant. I also enjoy the slightly minty but incredibly distinct fragrance of its foliage. They are short-lived in our climate but produce a huge punch when the weather is conducive. If we get too much rain during the spring, they melt. So planting these in containers or in raised beds during drought years is the best option, and planting them in the fall tends to be more ideal. There is one variety of petunia that has impressed me and it is Proven Winner's bubblegum supertunia. It is unbeatable in our area and handles the heat and humidity like a champ.

I love seeing bright orange and purple blooms with dark green foliage. LA lily hybrids are so fascinating to me, mixed with mystic spires salvia, upright elephant ears, and dianthus. It just screams tropical, and all of it comes back year after year. The combination is delightful. I try to plant things so at each time of the year I have some sort of interesting thing blooming or appearing. The colors I am most attracted to are the colors of wildflowers: yellows, whites, pinks, blues, reds, and purples. It brings me back to growing up in the mountains of Wyoming. It is hard to replicate the feeling where I am now, and I have had to learn a new appreciation for tropical colors.

Almond verbena and any variety of citrus tree are essential in every landscape. The blooms on citrus are the first to produce an intoxicating fragrance in the landscape, appearing at the end of March through June, followed by the sweet fragrance of almond verbena blooming June through the first frost. In the winter I love to plant hyacinths and paperwhites for mid-to-late-February blooms and fragrance.

What feeling do I want to experience upon driving up to my home? There is a German saying an old German man once shared with me: "If you want to see inside my soul, step into my garden." That is what I want to experience upon returning home. I want to feel full of life, love, protection, safety, nurture, and tranquility. Ours is the property that every creature in the surrounding 10-mile radius seeks out as a place of refuge, and they don't want to leave. We have a pair of bats who come twice a year during migration in the spring and fall. Our bird population is increasing annually. We have constant butterflies, bees, praying mantises, assassin bugs, lizards, geckos, dragon flies, crawdads, frogs, cicadas, and my favorite—tree frogs. Having frogs in gardens represents a healthy and fertile ecosystem. If frogs lay eggs, they consider your garden free of harmful chemicals due to herbicides, fungicides, insecticides, and synthetic chemicals found in fertilizers. When I see this kind of fertility, it sets my heart at ease. If all creatures are thriving, imagine what my family is doing.

The gardens in front of my house are not linear, neat, or orderly. They flow naturally together like God put the plants there by himself on purpose. I plant things that attract my heart and put them where they grow best. This is the hardest part of gardening, knowing each of the plants and what environment they thrive in. Even then, just like humans, plants will react differently to different environments. Even though we are composed of the same cells, we are all unique. I have moved almost every plant I have a time or two until they showed signs of thriving. To break it down in simple terms, if plants belong in the shade, plant them in the shade. The same is true for the sun. Never plant anything that is prone to fungus on the north-facing side of the house. The north side is most susceptible to fungus and algae. You can see this on trees, rocks, and structures where algae is most present. Plant items that are sensitive to cold on the south-facing side of the house. The house or structure will protect the plants from the bitter cold northern winds. Plant vegetable gardens on the south-facing side of the house. Plant herbs near a door where you can easily access them. If an area has poor drainage, plant water-loving plants. If an area cannot retain water, plant drought-tolerant plants. If a plant is visibly struggling after six months and not showing any signs of new growth where you have planted it, it's okay to move it to a different location. Pay attention to what the plant is telling you.

We are fortunate to live in an area in Southeast Texas where so many plants will grow. One of the major reasons I completely support local garden centers is for their incredible knowledge of the plants and what can grow here. It helps eliminate a lot of wasted time and money on trial and error. Another excellent source of helpful plant suggestions is from local botanical gardens. A wealth of gardens are at our fingertips, and each botanical garden has its own unique flavor. Each plant is selected for a purpose, and all are managed and nurtured using organic, sustainable practices. These gardens are designed to help plant enthusiasts like me find the right plants for my space and help create new inspiring ideas.

I have never seen a garden I didn't think was beautiful. Each garden is a free space to play with color, texture, and fragrance, to attract beautiful creatures, to gawk at the beauty of life. The only gardens I have not been attracted to are the ones that have been neglected. Even then, I still see their potential and know there is no lost hope. It's just like people. I am not attracted to people who don't take care of themselves, but I can see the potential in them with a little loving tender care. I cannot take care of everyone or everything; they need to do it for themselves. I can provide a hospitable environment for my plants and for my coworkers, friends, and family; however, it is up to them to see their own potential and grow from it.

Preparing the soil is the key ingredient for providing a healthy environment for plants and life to grow. For existing beds, this is an easy step. Each garden bed needs a border. If no borders are established, the beds will continue to grow farther out, making it harder to maintain. Borders can be made of metal, wood, rock, or brick. Since our soil expands and shrinks depending on moisture levels, and if there is no solid base for the border to lay on, the border will eventually get swallowed up by the soil. Adding 2 inches of compacted crushed granite makes a solid base for borders to be built on. Adding a thin layer of expanded shale and mixing it into the top 4 inches of the soil is also incredibly necessary. Expanded shale breaks up clay soils, allows for better drainage, helps retain moisture, and allows roots to grow deeper and wider. While adding the thin layer of expanded shale, I also like to add a thin layer of organic granular slow-release fertilizer filled with beneficial microbes, giving the life to your soil a jump start. The final step is adding 2 inches of compost to the top of the soil. Make sure you use a good compost, one that is not fresh and has been broken down long enough. Fresh compost has the potential to burn the plants. Compost adds live active microbes, breaks up soil, increases fertility, helps with drainage, suppresses harmful fungi, and provides a rich environment for healthy life to begin.

Now the fun and creativity can begin with the plants. You should have a little mix of everything in your garden. I like to begin with evergreen shrubs. Finding shrubs that grow to the desired height and width you would like lessens the input and maintenance of your garden. A few of the easiest shrubs to grow here in Zone 9a are Holly, Boxwood, Abelia, Japanese Yew, Camelia, Nandina, Viburnum, Ligustrum, Wax Myrtle, Cleyera, and Elaeagnus. Most of these, but not all, can tolerate both full sun and full shade. They will generally be the backdrop of your garden.

In the front flower beds that border my house, I have chosen to plant a variety of evergreen shrubs. My go-to shrub of choice is Nandina. They are slow-growing, and I have only a few clumps of them. Nandinas perform best with a little shade and are whimsical. I also have Dwarf Plum Yews because they remind me of the forests and landscaping of Wyoming, providing a woodlands feel that makes me feel at home. The Yule Tide Camelia I planted are for winter interest, which is when they typically bloom. The first time I saw these in real life was on a walk with my newborn around the holidays in the Heights in Houston. Their bright-red single petal blooms with a giant, cheery, golden center bring a smile to my face and heart. And my final evergreen is Mahonia media. This variety needs full shade because the heat and humidity become too intense for it. Its giant yellow fall blooms followed by large blue berries that look like grapes are so attractive to me and the birds. I love its unique rough texture, and it is very easy to grow, not requiring any special attention.

Shrubs and trees teach us patience. Planting them in fall or early winter is ideal. The first year of a newly planted shrub or tree is dedicated to spending most of its energy toward the development of the root system. There will be little to no growth above ground the first year. During the second year, the energy will be split between the root system and the above-ground plant. In the third year, you will see healthy growth above ground, which is a sign the roots are healthy and developed. It's kind of like relationships with people. Relationships should never be forced to be fully developed quickly. They take time, nurturing, and patience.

Armadillos love digging up my plants in search of bugs in the soil, especially when we are in a drought. Their favorite dinner is grub worms—June Bug larvae. They will tear everything out given the chance, but the few items armadillos, rabbits, and deer stay away from are plants with a strong fragrance such as Russian Sage, Mystic Spires Salvia, Artemisia (Wormwood), Lemon Balm, Rosemary, and Lavender. I mix those in with my plantings just to keep the armadillos out, but I also get the pleasure of using them and relishing in their beauty.

Rosemary is high in anti-inflammatory compounds and antioxidants that boost the immune system and improve blood circulation. Throughout history it has been used as the herb of remembrance because it improves memory performance and quality. It helps boost alertness and focus while also reducing stress and anxiety. Rosemary improves skin cells, works as a powerful anti-bacterial treatment, and aids in relief with digestive issues such as heartburn and liver and gallbladder problems. Obviously, it is often used in cooking, but I love to just have sprigs of it near me while I work.

Lavender is a challenge for me to grow here. But I still do. The varieties I have had the best results with are Spanish, Sweet, and Fernleaf. Do not plant this on the north-facing side of the house. I like to use it near beds when anyone in my house is having issues with sleeping. My favorite things to do with it are including it in a letter, tying it in the bow of a gift, or placing it in a vase mixed with flowers from the garden and nestling it by the bed for guests. Everyone says they always sleep so deeply when they come to visit, and I can't help but think the lavender in the vase by the bed has something to do with that.

I enjoy mixing perennials with herbs and annuals. Landscaping with kale, Swiss chard, and mustard greens in the winter is glorious. Mix them with flowering shrubs like roses, camelias, and azaleas. I refuse to amend my soil with anything other than compost, expanded shale, diatomaceous earth (DE), and compost tea. If the plants don't survive, then it's a no-go in my yard. Giving too much attention to a few plants takes away attention from the other living things at my house such as my hilarious family or my super-soft pets.

The key to choosing the right plant is to listen to your heart and intuition. If you are drawn to a plant for any reason at all, it was meant to be part of your life. There is always a reason, like the people who are put in your life at just the right time. Something draws us to certain people when our hearts feel safe and comfortable around them with just a few words spoken. The same is true for animals and plants. It is also pertinent to choose plants for their intended natural size. This will dramatically cut down personal input.

Once the front garden has been designed and planted, inspiration naturally begins to occur. Gardening is not meant to be rushed. It is a slow, mindful process. The plants will tell you what conditions they like if you just pay attention. It is not a big deal to transplant established plants to an area where they will thrive. And nothing is ever perfect on the very first attempt. Gardening is a continual process with no real end in sight, with constant change and so many things to learn. That is the exciting part. There are endless possibilities to what we get the privilege of learning.

❧

The Organic Lawn

Gardening is work, it is therapeutic, it is some of the best exercise you can do for yourself, it brings you closer to all of God's creation, and it gives you the strongest sense of self-accomplishment. It only takes one flower bed to get you started. My first flower bed was filled with a few evergreen shrubs, some perennials, a lot of annuals, and some vegetables and herbs. It was enough to give me encouragement and inspiration for other garden beds, and it satisfied my needs and wants until I had enough time, energy, and money to continue.

I spent so much time in my front yard, weeding, mulching, planting, harvesting, watering, daydreaming, getting lost in the beauty, and taking into account every little detail. I counted the new budding tomatoes and how many flower heads were emerging from my gorgeous, lush foxgloves. But at the same time, I was beginning to raise my family. I would plop my little one on a picnic blanket outside while I continued to garden. I didn't worry about what she was putting in her mouth or crawling around in. She was getting beneficial microbes into her gut through the soil. She was building her immune system and soaking up vitamin D through the sun's rays.

Synthetic chemicals are non-existent in our lawn. In September 2011 when the weather was finally cooling off only slightly in the evening, I became pregnant. That was when my whole life changed. Six months prior to the conception, I had a dream that I was pregnant. In the dream, I remember how clearly I knew I wanted to do everything I possibly could to have a healthy fetus. In the dream, I convinced my husband that we needed to move to the woods, grow our own food, and never use a microwave, TV, cell phone, or computer. I believed all those things would damage the fetus.

That was twelve years ago, but I still remember my whole life changing. Ms. Betty, the matriarch of the retail nursery I worked for, told her husband to make sure I didn't do any work on the computer while I was pregnant. She was concerned my child would suffer from spina bifida, a common birth defect affecting one out of every 2,000 births in the United States. It is a condition where an area of the spinal column doesn't form properly, leaving a section of the nerves and spinal cord exposed through an opening on the back. Betty had worked for several years as a medical technologist and had seen this many times. Her theory was that pregnant women who sat in front of the computer for several hours a day were most susceptible to this. Her theory only helped solidify the dream I had six months earlier.

Many years later, a sick-looking Himalayan female cat showed up at our house. I had her checked at the vet's office to see if she had a chip, but no. She was all mine, flees and ear mites included. I gave her a prescribed topical insecticide once a month for three months. I didn't know at the time that she was pregnant. When she had her litter, one of her kittens was born with spina bifida. She ended up eating the kitten. Was the spina bifida a result of the insecticide?

My morning sickness was an all-day event for the first seven months of pregnancy. Because of this I did not take the recommended daily multi-vitamin. Instead, I took folic acid and magnesium supplements only and would drink a probiotic drink every morning. I would also have a daily smoothie made with whole-fat Bulgarian yogurt. This not only gave me energy and eased my nausea, but the magnesium soothed my charley horses and helped me sleep at night. I also strongly believe the probiotic regimen was one of the reasons that Cheyenne's skin was healthy and strong and her bowels functioned properly when she was born. I did not have the same regimen with my second pregnancy, and she was born with constipation that she didn't grow out of until she was seven. Of course, I tend to blame myself for anything wrong with my children. Even though I know so much is out of my control, I have since come to terms with the reality that she just took longer to develop her bowel functions, just like her father when he was young. But part of me still can't help but believe the probiotics would have greatly improved her digestive tract and its development.

The point is, I wanted to nourish and protect my fetus more than I cared to do for myself before I was pregnant. Prior to my pregnancy, I did everything synthetically in my gardening practices. That was how I was taught when I worked at the garden center. Spray weed killer, spray fungicide, spray insecticide, and use fertilizer, and you will have a thick, green lawn and flower beds full of beautiful plants. However, I was spraying and inputting with very little satisfying results. I used four different lawn fertilizers a year, one major insecticide in late summer, one major fungicide in the fall, and one major herbicide in the spring. That is how I was taught that things were done here in Texas. At the garden center, we applied a liquid 20-20-20 fertilizer twice a week to all our plants through our water pump. When I became pregnant, the first time I watered with the fertilized water, I began to develop hives on my hands where the fertilizer touched. At first, I thought it was a coincidence, but when it consistently occurred with each watering, I finally put two and two together. A reaction like that caused me to become hyperaware of chemicals and the effects on my body. This was the moment when I feared for my unborn baby and what I was doing to her. I began my twelve-year research into alternative methods to fertilizer, herbicide, fungicide, and insecticide. This was the moment I became aware of my actions and their causes, not just to myself but to others and to all of us as a whole living on this earth.

Southeast Texas, south of the Houston area, has potential to provide a green lawn year-round. That is why lawn care is so incredibly relevant here. I was convinced I could control everything that occurred in my gardens and in my lawn, but like my child's gastrointestinal development, so much is out of my control.

While the grass is dormant and focusing growth on its root system in the winter, weeds begin to pop up in the compacted, poor-draining soils. It is difficult to find an herbicide strong enough to kill Texas broadleaf weeds and not cause damage to your lawn in the process. We suffer from intense heat in the summer, which will burn the lawn entirely if you use a strong herbicide at the wrong time of year. The most commonly used herbicides are Weed Beater Complete (granular) containing 2,4-D as the active ingredient, Weed Beater for Southern Lawns containing 2,4-D and MCPA (4-chlorine-2-methylphenozyatic acid), and Roundup containing glyphosate as the active ingredient. By now the whole world is aware of glyphosate and its potential for harm to the human body. But I'm not sure the whole world is familiar with the potential harm that 2,4-D has on the human body, animals, aquatic life, fertility, birth defects, and water. And I'm sure everyone is even less familiar with MCPA and its potential for harm in similar ways.

A farmer friend of ours just had a kidney removed because he was diagnosed with kidney cancer at the young age of forty. His wife said during our dinner, "Glyphosate causes cancer." Glyphosate is in most of our food, and I'm sure it is also in the food we feed our pets and babies. All three of these active ingredients in weed killers have potential harm for us, our pets, the microbes in the soil, the water table, and runoff into our streams and oceans. In small doses, our bodies (if the liver and kidneys are functioning well) filter out all these toxins. But we are subjected to toxins everywhere, from the lotions we use to the pollution in the air and added chemicals in our food. Using strong chemicals like these decreases not only the health but life expectancy of our pets, not to mention what it does to our own bodies, and the earth's body. I encourage you to do your own research on this topic and decide what makes the best sense for you.

As soon as we begin to see new growth from the sod, that's when we know there is above-ground activity and the grass is ready to begin taking in nutrients. This is the perfect time to fertilize the lawn. It's important to use a slow-release fertilizer with high-nitrogen levels. A fast-release nitrogen (ammoniacal nitrogen) product will encourage too quick of growth, leaving the new tender lawn more susceptible to fungal issues. If plants can't use all the nitrogen that is applied, bacteria in the soil will convert it to nitrates. Consuming water contaminated with nitrates causes many serious issues such as cancer in humans and pets. Seriously, I'm not trying to be fatalistic; I'm just telling it the way it is. In June or July, I typically added a fast-release, high-nitrogen fertilizer to green up my lawn from so much watering because it is so hot down here.

By the end of July through September, I applied an insecticide whose active ingredient was lambda-cyhalothrin (a synthetic pyrethrin). This was incredibly effective for killing arthropods (insects with an exoskeleton such as ants and chinch bugs) and every living insect imaginable, including our desperately needed pollinators. Chinch bugs would eat the tender new grass while their nymphs would feed on the roots just below the soil. I have seen chinch bugs destroy an entire lawn overnight. Where they attacked the lawns you could expect to have fungus known as brown patch or take-all patch in the fall.

Fungal issues begin to appear when the nights are cooler than 70 degrees Fahrenheit. Sometimes the fungus will not occur until November. Warm days and cool nights with high humidity are the perfect conditions for fungi to breed and thrive. It's an excellent time of year to go mushroom hunting here. Where we had drainage issues with the weeds in the spring and insect issues with the chinch bugs or army worms in the summer, brown patch was sure to rear its ugly head. Applying a granular systemic product with the active ingredient myclobutanil was common practice but not as effective as you would hope. Exposure to this chemical possibly causes issues with fertility and disorders in the development of the embryo or fetus, even if no signs show in the mother. There is a list of many more acute and chronic health effects.

As soon as growth ceases above ground, it was time for the grass to give energy to the growth below ground and time for one more treatment of fertilizer high in potassium (K), the last letter in N-P-K. N-P-K can be found on any fertilizer, for example 6-2-4 (4) is the amount of potassium. The higher the number the higher the concentration. Then we sit back for about two months and do it all over again, year after year with no signs of improvement or a lawn that could survive on its own without massive amounts of chemical applications.

With my newfound reason (carrying a life inside me) to pay attention to what I do and what chemicals I touch, I had to relearn everything I knew. This was the beginning of an uphill battle, all because I didn't want to have a baby with cancer or tumors or any other birth defects. I believed the fetus needed a fair shot at a healthy start in this world. The uphill battle was two-pronged: first, working in the horticulture industry with old ways of thought—chemicals solve everything—and second, changing the way I thought. I am no different than anyone else. Just recently I realized how much easier it is to take someone's word for it than to do research myself. It wasn't until the last four years, after COVID came about, that I realized how much trust I put in people in the medical field, without any questions. Now I have questions. With access to the Internet, I can find evidence for anything I choose to believe in, which makes finding truth that much more confusing. Instinct and logic are powerful and have always been a source I can trust. They have never let me down.

A few years ago, I decided I wanted to learn how to identify mushrooms in Texas. I wanted to be confident when foraging for one of God's most healthy and interesting creations. Mushrooms can be scary because there are highly toxic varieties. Southeast Texas has one of the most diverse fungal populations in the world. Of the 10,000 varieties growing here, over a hundred are toxic. I bought an excellent field guide for identifying mushrooms and had my first chance to put it to use just a few days ago in my own backyard. Growing under the oaks in the lawn, I came across gray-green-colored mushrooms. Quickly I grabbed *Texas Mushrooms: A Field Guide* by Susan Metzler and Van Metzler. After identifying the mushrooms as Russula virescens, which is not only edible but also considered one of the best in Europe, Asia, and North America, I confidently harvested all of them. But the mind is a mysterious thing. Had I bought these mushrooms at a grocery store in a container, I would have no doubt or fear at all about eating them. However, because they came from my lawn, it was scary for me to try them. I was 100 percent certain I identified them correctly, but I remained hesitant to try them. My kids and my husband were willing because they trust I know what I am doing. My intuition told me I had identified them correctly, but my mind was the only thing holding me back. Right there, standing in my yard with the mushroom in hand, I took a bite. Fresh mushrooms from the earth are much different than what you will find at the grocery store. The texture was slightly chalky and meaty at the same time, the flavor was smooth with a nutty aftertaste, and the whole experience was thrilling—along with the stories we all told the next day to our friends, coworkers, and children my kids go to school with.

Getting over the hump of prepackaged goods and trying

the gifts of nature should just come naturally, but it must be learned individually. It is something we are born with; however, as we become more educated and guided throughout our lives by outside resources, we become detached from nature's instinct and instead controlled by fear.

It's easier to just do what we are told rather than use our own intuition, minds, and objective thoughts. On a work trip visiting clients I would love to call friends in Lafayette, Louisiana, I witnessed the new natural way people live with one another. I found downtown Lafayette near the hotel I was staying at and wanted to try some local food and feel the local vibe. It was my first time in this town. There was an outdoor live music venue in the center of town, and a reggae band was performing later that night. I circled the venue five times. My soul was tugging me to go and jam out with all the Rastafarians and lovers of reggae. The music was mellow and happy. It reminded me not only of my times in college and my mixed tapes and CDs to pump me up before surfing when I lived in San Diego, but also of my one-day trip to Jamaica on a cruise with my husband. I picked up the dialect that day and still love being able to use it.

At the local restaurant where I ate, I could hear the reggae music, and my mind would not go anywhere else. A feeling of guilt overwhelmed me. Here I was alone in a city, seriously debating if I would really go to the concert while my husband and kids were home doing Girl Scout stuff and maybe not having the best time. I finished my amazing food and margarita and decided to circle the venue one more time. My heart and intuition said go, and I did. When the introduction for the band was being made, the announcer said, "Everyone stand up," and we all did. He said, "Everyone take your phones out and start videoing," and 92 percent of the crowd did. Where did living in the moment go? It is the new natural way—someone tells us to do something, and without thinking, we do it. The whole experience was wonderful, though, and I'm happy I went. But it did remind me of what the times look like now. I'm not trying to live in the past or make us go back to the way things were. I just want to help people reconnect with their hearts and intuition, absorb what is happening now, let go of what others think of them, and let their hearts and gut be their guide. Think before doing!

Organic Lawn Care

Weeds in the lawn typically begin to emerge in the winter in Southeast Texas when the grass has gone dormant. Most weeds show you there is a lack of calcium and phosphorus in the soil and usually higher levels of potassium. Where deep tuberous rooted weeds exist, you can be sure there is compaction. Weeds with deep roots are God's way of naturally breaking up compacted soil. The definition of weeds, whether good or bad, varies from person to person.

The first weed to emerge is native aster, usually around the end of summer until the first freeze. It is generally low-growing with a woody stem and produces tiny purple flowers. It grows best in full sun where the ground is compacted with poor drainage. I used to try to get rid of this weed when I lived in a subdivision where everyone drove past my house. The absolute only way to effectively get rid of it is to pull it, apply 1/4 inch of compost to the area, and water it in. Compost breaks up compacted soil, and if it's high in fungal content, it will deter weeds from growing in the area. As a seasoned gardener now, I love to leave aster wherever it so chooses to grow. It brings bees and butterflies to my gardens. The chickens eat their seeds, and they are sweet to look at.

As the grass begins dying even more, winter rye grass, chickweed, clover, and—if I'm lucky and it has been cold enough—real dandelions emerge. I love all these weeds. The winter ryegrass greens up Southern lawns in the winter and also assists with erosion control, retaining moisture, and the overall health of the soil by feeding the living microbes in the soil. My chickens love the seeds from ryegrass, supplementing their winter diet. Chickweed is also fabulous. Chickens love the tiny flowers and seeds they produce, and our family enjoys adding the freshly picked chickweed to our salads. It has been used in European traditional medicines for treating respiratory issues, digestive health by helping the kidneys function properly, and naturally suppressing the appetite. I have made a tincture of chickweed to assist in healthy bowel functions. It is magical and highly effective. Clover fixes nitrogen in the soil and attracts bees to the lawn. When clover is mowed, the nitrogen is released into the soil and acts as a natural fertilizer.

When COVID hit the world, my mind quickly became determined to figure out how to treat my family in case we came down with it since there was no treatment for this new virus. I spent a lot of my time praying because I had no control over anything and was struggling to wrap my mind around this novel virus that had the whole world living in fear and confusion. The news on the television and radio was very depressing, so after three weeks of nothing but COVID scare on the television, I turned it off and never looked back. God was my comfort, but I was still scared. Every morning and night for only a couple of weeks during breakfast and dinner, I forced my family to say three things they were grateful for. Eventually, we all began to be less scared. I still took moments to pray with my heart. That's when it hit me. God put all things on this earth for us to use. Everything has a purpose.

At first I thought it was just herbs that we buy at the store, and my mind grew more open to the herbs that grow wildly around here. That's when I discovered chickweed and its benefits. I was eating it from just about anywhere I could find it, but that was not a good idea. Now, I forage from my vegetable gardens. I know it hasn't been peed or defecated on, and the nutrients it derives from the soil are not laced with poisons from runoff near the road. I do not use herbicides, insecticides, or fungicides in, near, or around my house and property. But I do have five cats, one dog, eleven hens, and one rooster. We must not forget that all the animals in a 10-mile radius are attracted to our property for no reason other than the love and health our place emits. We don't typically eat off the ground unless it's mushrooms growing in just the right spot, but do not hesitate to eat straight out of the garden. Just wipe off the dirt and chow down.

Dandelions became another obsession of mine. Growing up in the mountains of Wyoming, dandelions and chamomile were my favorite weeds. They were so abundant. As a child, I picked the flowers all the way to the base of the stem, braided them together, and made a deep golden yellow dandelion crown for myself. My fingers would be stained from the bitter milky sap from the stems and from the flowers themselves. I didn't know you could eat them, but I truly enjoyed the bitterness of the milk, and licking the stems was such a fun thing to do. It was common knowledge that dandelions were used to make dye for clothes, so of course we tried to stain all our clothes by mashing the flowers up and down on whatever clothes we were wearing.

I'm pretty sure my mom used to sneak dandelion leaves into our salads, something I also enjoy doing for my family. The first time I snuck the leaves in our salad, I proudly announced that I had added a special ingredient to our salad and everyone must eat every bite. My husband asked if it was what he saw me picking in the ditch earlier in the day. It was, and I don't pick them from the ditch anymore, just around my gardens. Texas dandelions are not the kind you find in abundance in the North. The flowers in the South are a paler yellow with brown stamens, not deep gold; however, the leaves are very similar. The petals, leaves, and roots are edible. Pollinators love them, and they still have the same vitamins as the dandelions you find in the mountains. Dandelions cleanse the liver and kidneys, are loaded with antioxidants, and help regulate hormones. Absolutely fabulous stuff!

Frogfruit is another excellent multipurpose weed. It emerges in summer as a low-growing groundcover inhabiting full-sun areas with no need for irrigation. The blooms attract bees, and the leaves are used medicinally. When I had a nasty cough during COVID, I harvested and dried the leaves of this herb and made a tea. My cough was eased, and I felt better overall. Harvesting in the morning after the dew has dried up is the ideal time for herbs. This is the time of day they have the most oils and their potency is at its highest.

Wild purslane grows in the heat and humidity, usually in full sun. It works as an excellent groundcover and loves drought conditions. It is edible and highly nutritious. Wild purslane is best served mixed with salad or as the greens on avocado toast. It has the highest level of vitamin A of any green leafy vegetable.

As my knowledge has grown, weeds have become my friend instead of my foe. I see their value, even if I can't eat them. The blooms from all the weedy grasses and broadleaf weeds attract our native pollinators, wildlife, and birds, and each have their own purpose given to them by God. I accept them. I do, however, try my best to manage them. In lawns, having a thick thatch and deep hearty root system from the sod helps push the weeds out. It is the most effective weed control. Sod is much more aggressive than weeds, so making sure you have nutrient-rich soil is important, as well as good drainage and loosening compacted soils. Some weeds such as chickweed and purslane grow best in nutrient-rich fertile soil, and both of them are edible.

Nutsedge grows in moist-wet sunny soil. Identifying this grass is easy. It grows upright in your lawn faster than the sod.

It is triangular at the base of the grass, and if you follow the roots far enough, you will see a nut attached to more roots. It thrives in poorly drained areas. Pulling the weed can be difficult. If you don't pull it out gently and get the nuts attached to the roots, you will stimulate more vigorous growth. The nuts of the nutsedge are edible and quite tasty like a sweet tiny acorn. Having good drainage and applying horticultural molasses to the lawn will help reduce and eliminate the problem. Horticultural molasses attracts a beneficial worm that eats the nut of the nutsedge from the inside out. I used to have one garden bed at my old house where nutsedge was my main issue. I applied horticultural molasses to the bed, and within three months, I pulled up the nut, opened it, and saw a white worm eating the nut from the inside out. Applying molasses to problem areas not only stimulates microbial activity but also helps keep ants away. Ants can't stand the stickiness. Organic control is not immediate control, but it's the most effective for permanent elimination.

Having good drainage eliminates weeds. Applying a thin layer of compost over hard compacted areas also helps break up the soil and improves drainage, which allows the roots of the grass to grow more aggressively and push out weeds. Using humates (compost in a granular form) once every couple of years helps with the compaction. Apply humates in the fall—October or November—when you see the growth of the lawn decrease.

Proper maintenance is essential in weed control. For a St. Augustine lawn, mow it on a high level. You want the grass tall enough for it to shade the thatch. St. Augustine likes water, so irrigation is important. For Bermuda lawns, mow on a low level. Bermuda likes hot, dry conditions. Overwatering Bermuda will create an environment conducive to fungal issues.

Fungus is prevalent two times a year, usually in spring and fall when days are hot and humid and nights are cool (70 degrees Fahrenheit and below). This is also the best time of year to go mushroom hunting. Just like humans, when the immune systems of plants and grasses are compromised, they are more susceptible to viruses and struggle fighting them off without assistance. The best way to fight off viruses is to begin with a healthy immune system. Of course, there will be some cases where this is not necessarily true and additional inputs will be needed. The two most common fungal issues are take-all patch and brown patch. Take-all patch is a circular, yellowish-brown-colored patch, and when the grass is pulled up, the roots are extremely shallow or nonexistent. Brown patch is an actual circular brown patch in the lawn. Both viruses are a sign of an unhealthy immune system, poor drainage, excessive water, and alkaline soils. All of them occur naturally here.

For both take-all and brown patches, the first step is to remove any existing weeds in the affected area. The second step is to lay a thin layer of compost about 1/4 inch thick. Third, water it with compost tea. Only apply once in the spring and once again in the fall when necessary. For the past ten or so years, the importance of microorganisms in the soil has become an increasingly important topic. The soil is made up of so many living things, including mycorrhizal fungi and beneficial bacteria. These two things not only attack harmful fungi but also control the health and growth of the sod and plants. Adding compost tea is like adding intravenous probiotics to humans compared to a pill form of probiotics. In gardening, the pill form would come from a granular product containing mycorrhizal fungi. The beautiful thing about controlling bad fungus in lawns organically is that it builds the health of all plants and works to treat the problem and prevent it from reappearing.

Fertilizing only really needs to be done once or twice a year, depending on your interest. The truth is that you simply have to follow your intuition on this. If your lawn is looking healthy, don't fertilize. This could be the case for five years or more. When determining the best fertilizer for your lawn, there are some important environmental factors to take into account. Number one is the time of year. Fertilize in the late fall with a low nitrogen fertilizer and with something that helps break up soil and feeds the roots. Microlife Humates Plus is the best thing I have found so far for this task. Humates are the granular form of compost. Compost would be the absolute best solution for this project; however, it is neither aesthetically pleasing nor economical. If you want to make the commitment to get the job done right the first time, compost is what I would suggest. Compost breaks up the soil while adding beneficial organisms back into the soil. Fall is the ideal time to add a fertilizer that stimulates root growth—potassium (K). When finding the right fertilizer for this, look for a low nitrogen (N) variety that stimulates above-ground leaf growth, the first ingredient in the N-P-K; for example, 6-2-4. A low middle number phosphorus (P) stimulates some root growth and encourages blooms. Finally, look for high potassium (K), which stimulates root development and improves drought resistance.

Winter is the time for roots to grow. All plants and humans need time in their lives to stop the constant performance—time to withdraw and focus growth and energy on internal systems, our roots and organs. Doing this allows our systems to rejuvenate, refresh, and rebuild so we can continue the process of life all over again.

When plants and grass are stressed, they release a pheromone that attracts insects to attack it. That is why in the hot summer months you begin to see insect damage to the lawn. Insects are naturally occurring; they exist in both healthy and struggling lawns. The damage is only noticeable in lawns that are stressed and unable to support extra populations. The goal is to create a healthy lawn capable of bouncing back from damage caused by insects.

Determining which insect you have is the first step in proper control. There are only a few that cause severe damage. The first is chinch bugs. The damage is visible during hot, dry periods of summer in the hottest areas with full sun on the lawn. The damage begins to appear where there is soil compaction, usually by the driveway and sidewalks. It is also noticeable in dry spots of the lawn where there is significant compaction. Many confuse brown patch with chinch bug damage because they look similar. The difference is mainly time of year (chinch bug in the summer hot months and brown patch in cooler months when temperatures dip below 70 degrees Fahrenheit at night). When yellow patches appear in the lawn, water the area where the green grass meets the yellow grass in the evening (this is the time the insects are most actively feeding). You will see little black beetles with a silver bunny face marking (adult) across their backs begin moving up the blades of the grass. Those are your chinch bugs.

Chinch bugs can destroy an entire lawn in just a few days, leaving the damaged areas susceptible to fungal issues in the fall. They are a tiny bug whose body is exoskeletal (very hard and difficult to penetrate), which means they are difficult to kill. They also are rapid reproducers. Sprinkling organic food grade Diatomaceous Earth (DE) on the green areas surrounding the dead damaged areas of the lawn is quite effective at eliminating the insects. When their bodies move across the DE, it cuts up the chinch bugs, and they dry out and die.

Second is the sod web worm. They can be seen in late spring through fall, noticeable by the web spread over the lawn. They are the larvae of lawn moths. The moths lay eggs in the lawn where there is lighting at night. Once hatched, the larvae eat the sod, leaving long, empty strips of lawn looking like someone mowed strips at night while drunk. If you have a healthy bird population or chickens, you will never notice them, but if you need to treat it, apply DE.

Third is the fall armyworm, and just like chinch bugs and sod web worm, they are naturally occurring and don't cause damage unless you have an unhealthy lawn. The larvae of the fall armyworm moth are also attracted to areas with light at night. Again, a healthy bird population keeps this in check, so planting trees is an absolute must in your yard. Otherwise, use DE to remedy this situation, applying it when there is no chance of rain or water for a few days as it is water-soluble.

Healthy Lawn Maintenance

January–February: Weeds begin to emerge in areas with poor drainage or compaction. Lay a thin layer of compost on problem areas. Remove weeds in the affected area.

March–May: Make sure the blades on your lawn mower are sharp. Dull blades will tear the blades of the grass and make it more susceptible to disease. For St. Augustine, the first cut of the year will need to be about 1 inch shorter than the rest of the year. Scalping the lawn stimulates growth and loosens the thick thatch. The rest of the year, cut your lawn 3–4 inches high—the higher the better as the shade from the tall grass will act as a sun block for the roots and suppresses weed seeds from germinating. For Bermuda, cut shorter and often. Again, the first cut should be a notch or two shorter than the rest of the year, pushing it out of dormancy. The rest of the year, cut it 2–3 inches tall at least once a week until dormancy. This will help prevent disease. When new growth on the grass begins to appear, apply an organic fertilizer or humates. Distribution can be done by hand. Microlife (an organic fertilizer) contains beneficial microbes that replenish the soil health after using too much treated water. You will not burn your lawn if too much is applied to one area, unlike synthetic fertilizer. If you do burn your lawn by using too much synthetic fertilizer, the best way to remedy the situation is to leach your soil. Leaching is a process of applying massive amounts of water to flush the chemicals deeper into the soil.

June–August: St. Augustine grass likes hot, wet conditions, and Bermuda grass enjoys hot, dry conditions. The absolute best way to establish the lawn is to grow the roots deep so they can search out any available water, which minimizes the future input. Water it deep for thirty minutes. Wait thirty minutes and then water it again for thirty minutes. Do this once or twice a week until the lawn is established. Once your lawn is established, it is not necessary to water it, but it looks better if you do. It is important to pay attention to the conditions of the weather. In drought conditions, you may need to water more. However, like everything living, it is better to underwater than overwater. Fertilizing in the summer when the plant is constantly exhausting its energy or the soil is getting leached because of all the water, is an excellent idea. I love using a liquid fertilizer with horticultural molasses. Not only does the sugar feed the microorganisms but ants hate the stickiness and will leave your property.

September–December: Apply a thin layer of compost to problem areas. When the temperature cools down below 70 degrees Fahrenheit at night, apply compost tea to the areas where drainage is poor and damage has been done by either insects or fungi.

Inputs at year two should decrease by 25–50 percent. Lawn care requires the highest amount of chemical inputs and is one of the highest contributors to ecological pollution—polluting our water, including drinking water and our soils. My hairdresser confided in me that her husband had bladder cancer, and she was resolved to find the cause. She believes with all her heart that it was caused by the chemicals her husband religiously applied to the lawn. Converting to an organic approach greatly decreases the amount of poisonous runoff. Having strong, deep roots in our lawns decreases soil erosion. By using our clippings in our compost piles, we are feeding the beneficial bacteria that help our plants grow.

Lawn care is incredibly easy once you realize it's not the lawn you're taking care of; it's the soil. Lawn care was where I started on my organic journey. I began with the front appearance of my house—the front garden beds and lawn—because it was important to me to show everyone how much we cared for our house. I also wanted to make our neighborhood feel like a place that was cared for. I believe in the broken windows theory. If you leave a broken window unfixed, it encourages more crime and destruction in the area. The opposite is true with taking pride in your property or "The Pretty Yard Theory". All it takes is one neighbor to care for their lawn and flowerbeds, and the rest of the neighborhood will slowly but surely follow. There is a sense of pride we all take in our landscape. Planting beauty attracts people who appreciate beauty. I desperately enjoy walking in the neighborhood and looking at everyone's landscape. It never bores me no matter how many times I do it. Be the change you want to see.

Raised Bed Vegetable Gardening

Before I became pregnant, I did not care about my health. I smoked, drank a lot, and dabbled in drugs. When I had my first child, I was suddenly swallowed by fear—fear that I would take the job of being a mother as a burden, would be complacent, and wouldn't be strong enough for her. I was afraid she would be like the millions of other children with autism, cancer, birth defects, or learning disabilities. It's not that having a child with disabilities is the end of the world, but I would feel guilty like there was something I could have done to prevent it.

I thought of everything that could potentially cause an issue—cell phones, radiation from microwaves, exposure to chemicals from agriculture, our water sources, horticulture, and exposure to air pollution. But I did not think about vaccinations and if they played any role in the development of children. It wasn't even a consideration in my mind until my girls were nine and twelve. I just always blindly trusted that doctors were thoroughly informed about potential hazards of all things they put into our children's bodies via vaccines and drugs. I believed they were influenced by making our world a better, healthier place for our future generations. I still believe that to be true. No one becomes a doctor or pediatrician with the goal of harm. But I also think it is important to ask questions, fully understand what we are giving our children, and think about whether the benefits outweigh the risks.

Once I had my first child, my goal was to breastfeed for fourteen months, grow and make her food, and then have the healthiest baby ever. I wouldn't have to suffer the heartbreak of her dealing with immune issues. It's interesting to look back now and see that I thought I had all the control. In fact, God has the control, and to follow his direction, I must follow my intuition, do my part, and put forth effort. I wouldn't waste money on canned items when it was so much more efficient and economical to make and freeze my own food. That desire to give my daughter a fair first chance in life was still strong in me, and I took it one step further—to grow my own organic vegetables to use as baby food. We lived on a quarter acre, and most of our yard was in the front. I had very little room in the back to create a vegetable garden. My husband was on board and built me my first raised bed.

The material used to create a raised bed is the first most thoughtful step. We chose to use treated lumber. Other options included bricks, chopped rock, galvanized steel, rocks, or cedar. Previously, using treated lumber was strongly discouraged due to the toxins that would leach into the soil from the lumber. However, technology has once again come a long way, and studies show that vegetables grown in raised beds with treated lumber are not significantly affected by the chemicals used during the treatment process; however, you are the one who has to live with it so make the choice that's right for you. We have not had any issues with treated lumber, and I feel it is safe.

Before filling the raised bed with soil, place a layer of flattened cardboard directly on the ground. That prevents weeds from growing deep down below the few feet of soil by suffocating the weeds. Eventually, the cardboard will break down and become additional organic matter for the garden. It is not necessary to use high-quality soil when filling the bed, so for economic reasons use bulk soil and fill the bed to the top. Lay a thin layer of expanded shale on top. Mixing it into the top 6 inches of soil will allow for better drainage and aeration. Add 1 inch of earthworm castings to the top of the soil before adding 2 inches of compost. Earthworm castings are nature's fertilizer. They increase soil retention, feed microorganisms, develop stronger, healthier plants and fruits, and help fight off diseases. Doing this little step increases first-season vegetable production levels. It generally takes three years before the garden soil is rich and fertile. By adding 2 inches of soil conditioner by FoxFarm, you are dramatically speeding up the process of first-year production.

One spring I met a customer who was desperate to grow his own food organically for his family. His sixteen-year-old daughter had just been given a clean bill of health from a long, painful battle with cancer. When he was sharing his story with me, my heart began to squeeze itself, and I held back my tears. How scary as a parent to see your child suffer such a challenge at such a young age. They were a healthy family, ate healthy foods, exercised, and were good people. When their daughter was diagnosed with cancer, they couldn't figure out why or what had brought it on. I don't remember if she received chemotherapy or radiation, but I do know they sought an alternative holistic approach to treat the cancer. They went to a holistic doctor in New Mexico who had them reevaluate the way they consume, from the clothes they wear and the food they eat to the placement of the electrical box in their house.

She suggested they should not wear clothes that are fire-resistant (FR). It is common to find FR chemicals in everything from clothing to bedding to carpet. The food they ate could not be sugar-free or fat-free. They needed whole grains, whole fat, low to no sugar, and no sugar substitutes. If they couldn't understand or pronounce the ingredients on the package, they didn't need to eat it. Eating a vegetable-rich diet was encouraged. The electrical box in their house was on the outside of their daughter's bedroom, and they had it moved away from her wall because of the radiation it emitted. They washed their clothes with safe laundry detergent because the popular brands contained cancer-causing chemicals. Their daughter is now cancer-free.

The parents had a new perspective on what they bought

and how they ate. They were determined to grow most of their own food. They sought my advice on how to prepare beds and grow organically. The very first season of growing, they experienced an abnormally abundant crop. The one thing they added differently than what I suggested was a top-of-the-line soil for the top 6 inches of soil (Ocean Forest by FoxFarm). To really get a good head start, I suggested using 2 inches of FoxFarm's soil conditioner instead of compost. It usually takes two to three years of growing and nurturing the soil to have an abundant harvest like they had. They paid top dollar for high quality because the cost of poor health outweighed the money invested in gardening.

Raised bed gardens are an excellent way to begin the home veggie garden. They take less work and are easier to maintain. Weeds are a constant issue for gardens in the South. Weeds have been the reason I have given up on some of my gardens. They absolutely need to be controlled in gardens because they bring in insects, which bring in diseases and viruses. Having just a small area to weed is doable and even therapeutic. Raised bed gardens are easier on your back as well, with not as much need to bend over. Additionally, raised beds tend to be faster at production because their roots are not cooled off by the soil; rather, they are more exposed to hotter temperatures, making them develop faster. It is easy to overcrowd a raised bed. It is in our nature to want to produce a lot in a tiny space, but that goes against nature's law. Giving each plant ample space is pertinent to reaping a better harvest.

Watering is critical. Drip irrigation is the absolute best way to water everything. When water from sprinkler systems or a hose stays on the foliage of plants too long, fungal diseases begin to occur. The most common fungal diseases are powdery mildew, blights, and wilts. One of the easiest ways to prevent diseases is building your garden on the southern side of your house. It will be protected there from freezes and the susceptibility of northern exposure to diseases. Make sure the garden is in an area with plenty of airflow and do not overplant. Give each plant enough space to grow its roots comfortably. Plants, like humans, sweat through their foliage. When it's extremely hot, a nice shot of water cools off the plant, reviving it. Building the immune system by using compost tea four weeks after planting helps tremendously. Plants, just like humans, can fight off diseases and viruses naturally.

The year after I planted my incredibly tender cucumbers, we had warm humid days and cool nights. After two days, I lost half of my fresh transplants. I kept telling myself I needed to find time to brew some compost tea. I never found the time, and instead I continued to plant more new vegetables. I replanted my cucumbers by seed and put in tomato transplants, and both became infected. Again, I told myself that I needed to brew compost tea, and again I didn't make time. I worried I would lose those crops, too, but within one week they fought off the disease and left me with a theory that I had enough beneficial microbes already in the soil to build the immune system of the plants without my help. Or could it be possible that some years, different plants do better than others?

Gardens and plants grow when they are nurtured. Plants depend on us, and we on them. It is a symbiotic relationship—we cannot live without each other. The previous year, my vegetable garden was about spent at the first week of July. We left for a week's vacation. Upon returning, the garden was completely spent. I give a lot of attention to my gardens when I am home, once in the morning, and once in the evening, slowly walking through, counting the new blooms, killing the bad insects with my bare hands, pulling weeds, and harvesting ready crops. My garden thrives for me. Just like pets or children, if they know they are cared for, they thrive. I was gone for one week, and my plants gave up.

Crop rotation is crucial because it helps prevent disease. It is very hard to do that with just one raised bed. I utilized my flower beds for crop rotation and grew three to four different items. Incorporating large pots is also helpful in crop rotation. Some items that grow well in pots are tomatoes, peppers, strawberries, turnips, and greens like kale, lettuce, Swiss chard, and mustard and collard greens.

Raised beds are excellent for our area due to the unpredictable weather. Some years we wish it would just stop raining, and other years we pray it would just rain. Raised beds provide fabulous drainage in the years it won't stop raining; however, for the years it doesn't rain, using mulch (compost or pine straw) helps maintain the moisture.

When planning out the planting of the raised bed or

really any garden, planting marigolds is essential. Plant them in each corner of the bed. Marigolds attract beneficial insects such as ladybugs, lacewings, and parasitic wasps. But the most special quality is their ability to release a toxic chemical into the soil through its roots that kills nematodes. It is most effective in killing root knot nematodes that are attracted to the root system of the marigolds where they get trapped and are no longer able to continue their life cycles.

Insects in the Garden

Plants are so incredible. When plants are struggling, they release a pheromone that attracts insects to come and attack. If the plants have strong root systems with healthy microbial activity, the mycorrhizae fungi communicate to the root systems of the surrounding plants to strengthen them and build up resistance to the attackers. This is one way of fighting off insects from the soil level.

Living in what I like to call the Arctic jungle (when it's cold, it's bitter; when it's hot, it's unbearable), we are exposed to every insect ever imaginable, and they multiply quickly. Aphids, wooly aphids, scale, mealybugs, caterpillars, squash vine borers, pill bugs, leaf-footed stink bugs, stink bugs, flea beetles, spider mites, white flies, cabbage loopers, armyworms, hornworms, fungus gnats, ants, and cutworms are the most common insect problems in the garden. Making sure there is abundant soil health—created by adding mycorrhizae fungi through either compost tea, compost, or a granular form; proper air flow or ventilation; good drainage;

and adequate moisture—allows for the plants' immune systems to be excellent, resulting in better overall health.

This reminds me of Maslow's hierarchy of needs. The basic needs necessary for survival are physiological needs: food, water, rest, and shelter. These are the bottom tier, and things can only grow if these needs are met. Humans, plants, and all living things, including soil, require these physiological needs to fulfill their true potential. The second tier includes safety and security needs: knowing you'll get water and food when needed. The third tier is belongingness and love needs: having someone check on you regularly, pick the weeds, clean you up, kill the insects, and nurture you. These three tiers are the key components for a thriving population.

I spend real time in my garden. In the morning I walk through and look at everything. I see insects everywhere. The first week of April 2023, I was slightly discouraged by all the cucumber beetles mating and chewing on my gorgeous squash plants, but at the same time, I was encouraged by the amount of bees that were pollinating. Squash will open their flowers up in the morning at the same time bees are making their morning rounds. I love to hear the singing of the birds and the busy buzzing of the bees in the soft glow of the warm morning sun. Seeing all that life happening is soul-filling. I am still a human and have a hard time trusting both nature and God sometimes. I was really torn when I saw the cucumber beetles. That evening I almost treated the plants with a powdered form of spinosad, a product labeled at garden centers as organic. Spinosad works by attacking the insect's nervous system, whether by the insect ingesting it or even touching it. Essentially it is nerve poisoning. And it does not differentiate among insects. The evening is the appropriate time to do this type of pest control because the blooms are closed, leaving them guarded from the pesticide entering their reproductive parts, and harmful insects are feeding during the evening. But if a bee chooses to rest on a leaf that has been sprayed, that bee will die.

When I sauntered through my garden in the evening, I struggled with an internal battle of whether or not to use insecticide. I examined the plants, and even though there was a clear infestation and the population was increasing daily, there was no damage to the plants, the fruits, or the flowers. As my foreman back in my diesel mechanic days taught me, "If it ain't broke, don't fix it." I have seen with my own eyes the miracles of nature and God, and I let it be. But there is nothing wrong with adding a little Western medicine to assist in extermination. My stroll in the garden the next morning was more disconcerting. It was as if every cucumber beetle had twelve babies of their own, and every one of them was mating. I had both varieties of flea beetles in my garden—black with yellow stripes and yellow with black stripes. Out of panic I applied Spinosad to the veggies while the blooms were open for the bees. Every year is a different issue.

Spring of 2024 was the year of the worm. One morning I stepped outside to see my mulberry tree completely covered by web worms. My husband wanted to spray something—anything. I told him we should just let it be and see what happens. The web worms completely defoliated my mulberry tree, but it put new healthier growth on quickly. The web worms gave the tree a much-needed buzz cut so it could be healthier. Gardening keeps things interesting and becomes a continual learning process. While I was doing yoga and reflecting, my heart sank to my stomach. I realized that I didn't trust myself, my instincts, nature, or God. In the back of my mind, I heard a voice saying, "Give yourself grace." As soon as I returned home, I washed away the poison I had applied to the plants earlier.

Insect infestation has always happened in my gardens. It happens in every garden I have seen. It is a natural occurrence. But plants are resilient like earth and humans. If we have a strong immune system, we can fight off anything. I let fear of a pathogen guide me hastily, and I took control of it rather than letting things play out. Gardening is a constant reminder that I don't know everything, and there is so much to learn. I have no control, I must practice patience, and I have to remember that everything happens for a reason. I must have faith that all the living things around here will not only survive but thrive. Insect infestations are difficult to just let occur. Every disease possible will happen at one time or another in this part of Texas. It is a breeding ground for fungi, insects, viruses, and diseases. It's the jungle. You truly have to be strong to survive and trust your instincts when it comes to control of issues. All of life is black and white, yin and yang, good and bad, sad and happy. One cannot exist without the other. I made the right decision using the insecticide. I have lost crops due to disease by letting things play out, but it is not worth the feeling of guilt. That's why I am constantly learning new organic approaches to insecticide, and a diatomaceous earth spray is the solution.

Diatomaceous Earth Spray

- 32 ounces of water
- 1 tablespoon diatomaceous earth
- 1/2 teaspoon Dawn dish soap

Mix all ingredients together in a spray bottle, shake well, and apply to top and bottom of foliage.

The internal struggle I faced regarding using manmade chemicals in my garden or letting the plant struggle and heal on its own is the same struggle I face when either my children or I are ill. I want to stick with natural instinct first, using the gifts from the earth put here by God, always remembering to say my thankful prayers. When that fails, if it fails, I use Western medicine. Who said only one kind of medicine is right? Eastern or Western? Who ever said only one God is the right God? In every culture from the dawn of time, people have had faith in something they cannot see, which is much larger than themselves, all-powerful, able to create miracles, and omnipresent. And the basis of every religion is the same. Do unto others as you would have them do unto you. Be kind. Love one another. God creates gifts of the earth for us to use at the appropriate time.

For example, when my family and I went camping in September 2020, the day we showed up at the campsite we all came down with COVID. That was really something. It hit us hard, and we were unprepared. We had stocked up on vitamin C and zinc, but all that was at home in our cabinet. After the first day, I convinced my family to get up and go for a 3-mile hike to forage for something to give us relief. Halfway through the hike and after passing several already fruited prickly pear cacti, I found one prickly pear cactus shining in a field with several fully ripe fruits. We harvested and made prickly pear French press tea back at the campsite. It gave us all temporary relief and enough vitamin C to give us energy to swim in the San Marcos River.

Throughout my years of gardening, I have learned the implementation of trap crops to control insects. The leaf-footed stink bugs were my first greatest nemesis. They will destroy a tomato crop in a matter of three days. Their eggs are distinctly light brown to gray colored and are usually laid in a columnar line—like barrels stacked on one another—on or near the host plant. This is the best time to take matters in your own hands. Kill them at this point because once they hatch, you will likely be dealing with hundreds of nymphs. The first year I saw the nymphs, I confused them with the beneficial insect the assassin bug. I let them live, and they quickly destroyed my beloved tomato crop. When they are nymphs, they are easy to kill by squishing them with your fingers. Wearing gloves helps take away the grossness of this process. When water is applied to the plant, the nymphs move upward and are easy to locate. Once they become adults, your crop will be demolished almost overnight. They have a stinger nose that penetrates the tender skin of the tomato, forcing it to mature too quickly. I accidentally stumbled across a beautiful way to protect my crop without using chemicals or too much manual labor. After planting artichokes to increase the fiber in our diet, I realized the leaf-footed stink bug was much more attracted to the artichoke plant than any other crop I had. Cardoon artichokes and sunflowers should be planted away from your garden to deter insects from any wanted crops.

Tomato hornworms are another naturally occurring issue. When I first discovered them in my garden, it was during evening feeding time. I love counting the tomatoes I can expect to receive in the future. It brings me a sense of accomplishment knowing I am growing some of nature's candy for my family, and it builds my self-esteem. Nothing tastes sweeter than vine-ripened tomatoes. A true plant-lover gets close and examines every detail of the plant. If it is quiet enough, you can hear the chewing of the caterpillar, which makes it easier to locate, remove, and squish. If I find them, I feed them to our chickens. Natural predators are birds. Attracting birds to your garden is not bad. They will typically leave the fruit of the tomatoes alone if there is ample water supply nearby. The only reason they will attack the fruit of the tomato is to get the water out of it. Not all birds like still water; some enjoy moving water, so having both a bird bath and a fountain will assist in a healthy functioning system. The birds prefer eating insects over tomatoes; however, that is not necessarily the case with fruits and berries.

Another effective trap crop is mustard greens. They are incredibly nutritious and make a spectacular display of foliage from early fall to late spring. Flea beetles and aphids will be more attracted to mustard greens than other fall vegetables. A wonderful woman named Kim introduced me to fermenting mustard greens. There are many ways a person can utilize greens. The favorite for my family is Southern mustard greens as a side dish.

This dish is so concentrated in nutrition it is unbelievable. The abundance of minerals and nutrients will stop a cold dead in its tracks after only one meal. It's amazing that God allows certain plants to grow at the same time they are needed for healing. It's the perfect side dish to serve during the beginning stages of colds and flus, or when the immune system needs a boost. Greens are ready for harvest during the coldest months of the year (November through May) when kids are getting sick at school and we have many family gatherings. I've noticed that it's usually during the holidays when people are gathering often that illness becomes pervasive.

Mustard greens are an excellent source of fiber, which increases the flushing of bad viruses, bacteria, and blood cells out of the body. The greens contain a high source of vitamin C (antioxidant), vitamin K (helps build bone mass and protects against brain damage caused by Alzheimer's disease), and vitamin A (assists in healthy skin and protects against lung and oral cancers).

Mustard greens are also fundamental for using as a trap crop. When the weather is hot and dry during fall planting, flea beetles and aphids will be more attracted to the mustard greens than any other crop, and mustard greens bounce back quickly after being eaten to the ground. Whichever row I use to plant my mustard greens, that will also be the row I plant my potatoes in December through January. Mustard greens manage the soil-borne pathogens such as fungi and pesty nematodes. Florida broadleaf mustard greens are by far the easiest and heaviest producer for consumption and trap crop.

Sunflowers are easy, beautiful, and a necessary trap crop to attract beneficial insects, bad insects, and birds. Their giant sunny flowers brighten every garden with edible seeds. Cutting off the giant heads after the petals begin to wilt is the best time to harvest the seeds. Let the seeds dry while they're still on the flower in full sun for a couple days, and then move them indoors to finish the drying process. Once the seeds have fully dried, remove them by breaking open the flower head and taking a deep breath of the sweetest floral fragrance you have ever had a chance to encounter. Sunflowers act as a perch for birds, allowing them to scout the garden for delicious insects. As mentioned before, birds will only eat vegetables if there is no water for them to consume, so having a birdbath and some flowing water from a fountain or anything else will help keep the birds off the vegetables.

Another excellent plant used as not only a trap crop but also as medicine is nasturtium. The blooms have a floral peppery flavor and can be eaten fresh in salads or off the vine, or can be used as a decorative edible flower on trays of deviled eggs. The flowers, foliage, and seeds have all been used medicinally in teas and tonics to treat internal infections, provide immune system support, and heal respiratory issues such as coughs and sore throats. Planting them in the fall is ideal. They will die back in freezes, but if you let them be, they will come back in early spring, just in time to heal coughing from allergies. I use the leaves on my avocado toast. The creaminess of the avocado mixed with the slight crunch and pepper flavor of the nasturtium leaves are the perfect combination. Adding leaves to a tea works like a natural cough suppressant.

Nasturtium is used as a trap crop. Leaf miner, aphids, and all sorts of beneficial insects are attracted to this plant. It is also beneficial in repelling stink bugs and cucumber beetles. In 2023, I did not plant any in my in-ground garden, which may be the reason I had such a horrible infestation. Citrus and roses are particularly susceptible to leaf miner, which only creates a superficial aesthetic issue and are not damaging to crops.

❧

Food as Medicine

Viewing food as medicine began for me in college about twenty-four years ago. My head was not in a healthy place, like most people who are on their own trying to figure out their place in the world. Raised in a family of divorce and dysfunction spurred a lack of self-confidence and self-love. I found my peace and moments of clarity when I was hiking in the mountains, walking in the neighborhoods spying on other people's gardens, and visiting bookstores. In 2002, I found a book called *The Healthy Kitchen: Recipes for a Better Body, Life, and Spirit* by Andrew Weil and Rosie Daley. The book opened my eyes to viewing food as medicine. All those years my mom forced our family to eat doll and seaweed, brown rice, and every type of fish now became understandable to me.

Using healthy fats our bodies can naturally process such as first cold-pressed olive oil and full-fat instead of fat-free, not only helps our metabolism but also cushions our cells and protects them from harmful invasions such as cancer and other diseases. Lipids (fats) protect our cells from damage and are also the substance for communication among cells. The book taught me that having carbohydrates in our diet is important for providing energy the body uses for everyday function and physical activity. Protein is necessary to make and maintain healthy tissue but should not be the primary food we consume. Vegetables should be one of the most highly consumed items in the diet. At the very end of the book there is a section about chocolate and its health benefits. Chocolate, when it is high-quality and its first ingredient is cocoa butter or chocolate liquor instead of sugar, has powerful healing qualities. High-quality chocolate usually has the percentage of 70–78 percent cocoa. With a high-quality chocolate, your body can process the cocoa butter easily like it would olive oil. It assists in cardiovascular health, has strong antioxidant activity as much as red wine and green tea, and can act as a rapid-acting antidepressant. Having this information made me look at all food items in a new light and made me think for the first time about what kinds of food I was putting into my body.

The book inspired me in many ways. The first (creatively) was to throw a Mediterranean birthday dinner party for a sweet friend of mine. Spending the whole day creating something new to eat and share with my friends was exciting. It allowed me to get out of my ego and just enjoy the gathering of wonderful, interesting, hilarious people. We drank, we laughed, we jammed out to music, and we enjoyed food together. That book created an evening of medicine for the soul, not just for me but for everyone involved. Because of that evening, a new inspiration—food—grew within my group of friends. Danny, a first-generation college student, was there. He had veered from the path of a bull-riding Wyoming cowboy life to creating amazing dishes he shared with me and his future wife frequently. The most memorable was his butternut squash soup with homemade croutons. I still replicate his recipe once a year.

Second (inspirationally), I was inspired to grow herbs indoors to use for fresh cooking. In Wyoming, growing herbs inside is possible, and growing veggies or herbs outdoors has only a three-month window. I tried and failed with the herbs, but it was a necessary steppingstone for indoor plants.

Third (therapeutically), the newfound knowledge has been at the base of most of my decisions concerning food and began my creative process for making my own food, including my now six-year-old sourdough starter, Frances Jean, and fermented veggies in a crock. The introduction of microbes is a fairly recent journey, one that started in the last eleven years.

Butternut Squash Soup with Croutons

- 1 butternut squash
- 1.5 cups heavy whipping cream
- 6 cups chicken bone broth (I make my own—very easy)
- 3 large carrots, peeled and chopped

- 1 large onion
- 2 celery ribs, chopped
- 3 tablespoons olive oil
- 2 tablespoons butter
- 3 cloves garlic, chopped
- 1-1/2 tablespoons chicken bouillon
- 1 tablespoon cardamom
- 1 tablespoon coriander
- 1 tablespoon cumin
- Salt and white pepper to taste

Preheat oven to 400 degrees. Wash butternut squash, cut off both ends and stab skin with a fork all over. In a dish lined with parchment paper, bake in preheated oven for 20 minutes. Remove from oven and peel.

Peel and chop carrots, celery, and butternut squash into cubes. Dice the onion. Combine these four ingredients in a large pot or Dutch oven with 3 tablespoons hot olive oil. I prefer cooking with either cast iron or stainless steel. Cook over medium heat for about 15 minutes or until squash has softened. Add the 2 tablespoons of butter at this point.

Once the vegetables have softened add the chopped garlic, cardamom, coriander, and cumin. Cook for 1 minute. Add bone broth and bring to a boil, add chicken bouillon, cover and let simmer for 30 minutes, stirring occasionally.

Add heavy whipping cream, and with an immersion blender, blend everything together. Add salt and pepper to taste or add more spices to satisfy your pallet. Serve with a dollop of sour cream and croutons.

Homemade Croutons

- Half a loaf of rye bread, diced (any kind will work, but homemade sourdough tends to become hard like a brick. I encourage bravery and trying new things at all times.)
- Salt
- Pepper
- Four cloves garlic, chopped
- Any herbs you are currently growing (chives, parsley, mint, oregano, basil, thyme, sage, winter savory) except rosemary, chopped
- 3 tablespoons olive oil
- 3 tablespoons melted butter

Preheat oven to 375 degrees.

Combine all ingredients in a large bowl and mix together with your hands.

Lay out flat on a baking sheet and place in oven for 15 minutes, flipping croutons halfway through.

Remove and let cool. The croutons can be stored in a container in the refrigerator for up to 10 days.

Chicken Bone Broth

- Use the bones of three chickens.
- 4 whole quartered onions
- 1 pound peeled carrots cut in half lengthwise
- 6 cloves of garlic, peeled
- 3 celery stalks plus greens
- Salt

Combine all ingredients in one giant pot; fill to the top with water; cover and bring to a boil.

Reduce heat to low and simmer for 12–24 hours. Add more water if needed during the simmering process.

Let cool, strain, and place bowls of broth in fridge for 24 hours.

Skim off and discard fat from the top of the broth.

Measure out freezer bags of 1 cup, 2 cups, and 6 cups of broth.

Freeze up to 6 months. Use in all recipes for added minerals, nutrients, and flavor.

Bone broth is rich in nutrients such as iron, vitamins A and K, fatty acids, selenium, zinc, manganese, calcium, magnesium, and phosphorus. The collagen from the bones provides amino acids, protects the wear and tear of joints, and reduces inflammation. Bone broth protects the gut, aids in weight loss, increases cardiovascular health, and promotes better sleep.

When my youngest daughter was at the age of trying foods (six months), I could not get her to eat my nutrient-dense homegrown, cooked, and frozen baby foods. I was desperate to get her interested in food so she could get the needed minerals and nutrients. Then I discovered bone broth. Adding it to the vegetables I smashed for her was a huge success. It calmed my heart knowing I was giving her the nutrition her body needed, and it greatly improved the nutrition for the entire family. In a way, she saved us.

Food as medicine proved its value when my amazing friend Sarah was diagnosed with lupus. She was forced into early retirement from her career in the United States Air Force because of this condition. Lupus is an autoimmune disease that occurs when your body's immune system attacks its own tissues and organs. There is no known cure. The doctor sent her home with a bag full of several medications to help relieve the side effects of the disease such as skin rashes, fevers, pain, and flare-ups of the joints. Sarah, who had a BA in history, was a devout researcher and believed there had to be an alternative for all the medications she was given. She began her research for an alternative to the medications for autoimmune diseases.

Diet and lifestyle change was the highest recommended. She had always been very conscientious of what she put in her body. Until that day, she had eaten a low-fat, sugar-free diet and exercised. She felt she took very good care of herself. Through her research she discovered that the good she thought she was doing for herself was actually slowly killing her. Food companies often replace the fat in low-fat and fat-free products with sugar, which feeds cancer, viruses, and bacteria, and causes inflammation. Food companies also replace the sugar in sugar-free products with synthetic chemicals. Our bodies are designed to process food items that contain fat and naturally occurring sugar. Our bodies are not as capable of processing synthetic materials.

My inspirational friend was tired of hurting, and because of her incredible determination, bravery, and strength, she changed the way she viewed food that day. Six months after the doctor sent her home with a bag of medications, Sarah returned for a check-up. Her doctor was elated to see the medications had sent her lupus into remission; however, Sarah had never once touched the medicine. Instead, she had changed the way she ate. I have always been impressed with her strength and personal resolve. She has a gorgeous garden and produces and cans almost her whole diet. Oddly enough, she now enjoys collecting pressure cookers. You just never know. Fifteen years later, her lupus was still in remission, and then her employer forced her to take the COVID 19 vaccine, which caused everything to flare up worse than ever before. Unfortunately, her doctor would not sign off to allow her to opt out of the vaccine due to her underlying health issues.

I remember visiting Sarah at her house in Las Vegas. She

opened my eyes to a different point of view. The first thing we did when I arrived was go to the grocery store where she busily talked about her new diet, pointing out the ingredients in every packaged item and making special note of the amount of sugar. We made it to the fruit section where she picked up every lime, touching, squeezing, smelling, and thoroughly visually inspecting each one. She had a mission: teach me everything she learned through months and months of research.

The most wonderful moment of the trip was the incredible welcome feeling I received from her. She allowed me into her house and showed me her soul. The bold bird's nest blue color of the entrance walls contrasted perfectly with the eccentric burnt orange color of her living room. Her freedom and bravery in her color choices were so refreshing. We spent the afternoon making freshly squeezed lime juice for our margaritas, the only margaritas I will drink now. They're to die for! We ate clean the entire time I visited her. The feeling stayed with me. I felt better about myself and was inspired to care for myself after leaving. It's been fifteen years since I visited my dear friend, and I still recall what we ate: steak from pasture-grazed cows with melted butter, milk with a layer of fat on top, real yogurt, summer squash, escargot, guacamole, tortilla chips, and gelato.

Sarah had the funds to eat clean. I didn't think I would be able to afford to do the same. Little by little, making better choices, I realized it was not that much of a difference. Now it is even more balanced, and there are local farms where you can purchase grass-fed meat, chicken, beef, or pork for a reasonable price. The visit felt more like an awakening. Most of our time was spent drinking and eating, some antiquing, and a visit to a reflexologist. That is where I discovered the healing powers of pressure points on the feet.

Historically, using pressure points to heal has been documented from as far back as 12,000 BC in Latin America with the Incas to 2330–2500 BC in Egypt. In every culture around the world it has been used to treat all varieties of ailments. I remember when I was young and had a headache, my mom would tell me to squeeze the soft spot between my thumb and forefinger on both hands to relieve the pain. It worked then and continues to this day. Just recently, my friend and I spent our birthdays together at a reflexologist in Houston's Chinatown. The minute they began their work on our feet, my stomach started rumbling and my sinuses cleared up. I concentrated on what I felt inside and where I felt it as the pressure points were being stimulated. The body is an amazing thing.

What Sarah did was incredibly difficult for most people, including me. It's scary to believe that medications aren't always the answer and that an actual life change is. It wasn't just changing her diet; it involved an emotional and spiritual change as well. Making a conscious effort to change ourselves and our perception of what is best for us is the hardest part. It's important to try to practice the natural remedies before resorting to medication. What makes trusting nature difficult is having to trust God.

As humans we are inclined to need proof, scientifically measured evidence of nature working correctly. I am that way, and it is an internal struggle I have. I attended an eight-hour class taught by Dr. Elaine Ingham on the Soil Food Web. As a gardener, I can see when my plants are struggling, look sick, or look like they are thriving. And I just know it for sure if I have a problem or not without having to dissect everything. But when I do dissect and can visibly see for myself what is occurring with or without a microscope and see with my eyes life at work, then I feel confident in my beliefs. Before I saw the microbes in the soil with my own eyes under a microscope, I knew they were there and had a purpose. But once I saw them, I was filled with excitement and inspired to help facilitate in strong healthy microbes for stronger healthier plants and people.

Beneficial Microbes

Microscopic microbes inside and outside our bodies have a symbiotic relationship with us. Ultimately, if we take care of the beneficial microbes, they will in turn take care of us. They are the cause of our immune system and determine how well we fight off viruses and diseases. They are also the cause of mental health. This world of microbiome includes bacteria, fungi, viruses, archeae (they look similar to bacteria but are entirely different), and helminths (nematodes). The quality of our lives is determined by the microbes that live in us and on us, and it matters how well we take care of them. The same beneficial microbes can also be found in our soil and are the immune system for our plants.

We begin building our microbiome when we are born. If our babies are fortunate enough to go through a vaginal birth, their skin gets covered by the beneficial microbes from their mother to help protect their tender skin in a whole new foreign environment. This was the function God created our bodies to be capable of. The milk mothers produce also builds the microbiome in the guts of their babies. When we sweat, the moisture we produce mixes with the bacteria on our skin to create an odor, not the actual sweat. Microbes work with us and are a part of us from day one. We need them and they need us to survive. It's the microbes that help us heal and rebuild damaged cells. The microbiome in our guts help digest the food we eat and the liquids we drink. Without them, we do not function properly.

Microbes found in the human body, in the ocean, and in the soil are all very similar. The human body, ocean, and soil can heal themselves. This thought has given me comfort when I hear how we're damaging the oceans, our water sources, and ourselves with the chemicals and microplastics everywhere. There is so much doomsday talk and so much fear being spread because fear controls human emotions and drive. All that helpless talk is depressing, especially for those raising children or have grandchildren. No wonder so many people are walking around with anxiety and fear when that is what is being fed to us. Where is the hope for the future? Hope lies in the ability to heal, which is a superpower given to us by God.

If we live a little more gently and with nature rather than against her, we can heal all at the same time. If we stop putting toxins in our bodies or stop relying on antibiotics every time we get a cold, our cells will have the opportunity to rebuild and heal. The first time I heard about the symbiotic relationship between plants and microbes, everything changed about how I gardened. Now I garden to feed and protect the microbes, which then feed and protect the plants while at the same time getting the microbes osmotically through our bare feet and hands for my gut health and the gut health of my family.

When I first began gardening in Texas, Cassia, an incredible woman I worked with, encouraged me to try planting with leaf mold compost. Dig the hole twice the size of the plant, add a large handful of compost in the hole, plant the transplant, and finally use the compost as the mulch around the base of the plant. Without adding anything else, the plant grew and thrived better than what I had previously tried. If it worked so well for the individual new plants, what would it do for the existing plants? Using compost as mulch rebuilds the soil structure, helps with water retention, assists in drainage by breaking up compacted soils, and adds beneficial microbes back into the soil.

It is important to find high-quality compost rich in microbial activity and without pathogens. At first I bought compost by the bag, but this is not economical for how much I use. That is why it is so important and so easy to have your own source of compost.

Compost

What makes a high-quality compost is the material (brown matter, green matter, and microbes), water, and aeration (oxygen flow). Compost can be made and completed in twenty-eight days if done correctly. I take a much more relaxed approach and still have fabulous quality. The base layer is the organic waste material (poop). I don't like to use livestock manure because of the heavy salt content. Luckily, we have chickens. I allow the poop to build up in the chicken coop, which I cover with layers of fine pine shavings from the feed store.

Twice a year we clean out the coop and make two piles of compost. We add our old compost, dried leaves and branches of trees and shrubs. The final layer is the food for the microorganisms, green material. We use grass clippings and the vegetable plants that have finished growing. To give the microbes a quick start, add a handful and a half of microbial inoculant (easily found at any local garden center) and water everything really well. Using city water or treated water will kill the beneficial microbes. Capturing rainwater or using well water solves this problem. Every seven to ten days, flip the pile using a pitchfork, a tractor, or an auger attachment for a drill by Power Planter. Warning: Depending on how much of which material you use, the pile can catch fire. We have seen our pile steaming in the middle of summer. That is hot!

I have tried and failed to use a compost tumbler. It gets too hot without enough airflow for our area. The best success I have had is to make a pile somewhere hidden in our backyard where it receives ample shade and is able to get wet when it rains. During drought years I water my piles when needed. You don't want it too wet—just enough to keep things cooled down and moving.

It took about three months for us to finally get an active healthy compost pile going. I knew it was good by the smell. The intense fragrance should be made into cologne. It's deep and sweet, earthy, and spicy with a touch of floral. It reminds me of a clean, fresh man mixed with hot herbal tea made with spices like clove and cardamom. I love the smell. And it's a fun party trick of mine to have company walk to the compost pile and take a big whiff. One of my friends says it smells like rain, but to me it is so much more complex. Breathing it in calms my spirit. The color should be a dark, rich brown and the texture fluffier than soil.

Until recently when I bought my microscope, I wasn't sure how much activity was taking place in our piles. They have everything from mycorrhizae fungi visible with the human eye to bacteria and nematodes. I use the compost and see the results of healthy plants and ecosystem, and seeing through the microscope gives me reassurance. The magic of compost is its microscopic world of living organisms. The bacteria, mycorrhizae fungi, and nematodes protect roots of plants from pathogens and parasites, break down nutrients in the soil, and transport the water and nutrients to the plant. They are also the communication among the plants.

There was a book I was incredibly drawn to in college, *The Tao of Pooh* by Benjamin Hoff. I have spent so much of my time trying to figure out the why when the answer is Cottleston Pie. Things are the way they are just because. Things are the way they are exactly the way God intended. God didn't make animals to take care of us, he didn't make plants to take care of us, and he didn't make microbes to take care of us, yet they all do. He created us to take care of all living things, and in return, they give us health and nutrition. It's simple. The proof of all things working together is something you can feel through your body when working in the garden, touching, smelling, visually soaking up the colors, and seeing life all around, observing what actually exists and not what people tell us exists but what we experience in real time. What we observe with all our senses is what really exists.

Excellent items to add to the compost pile:

- Used tea (loose leaf) and their bags (if they are not plastic)

- Crushed eggshells (adds calcium)
- Fish bones or shrimp shells (adds calcium)
- Vegetable peelings or rotting vegetables (nothing that has been cooked in butter or oil)
- All fruits, including citrus peels
- Shredded paper
- Wood ash
- Trimmings from shrubs (if woody part is too large, chop into much smaller pieces)
- Untreated lawn trimmings (without pesticides, herbicides, or fungicides) (that is what feeds microorganisms)
- Chicken, horse, and a little cow poop are all good (where the microorganisms come from)
- Comfrey (adds naturally occurring fertilizer and has measurable N-P-K)

Do not add the following items to the compost pile:

- Baked goods (pasta, tortilla, bread)
- All animal parts
- All things dairy or made with oil
- Plastic
- Diseased plants

- Oleander (if not composted thoroughly, plants will absorb the deadly chemical (oleandrin) produced by oleander and can be detected in plants grown in its compost)

Compost Tea

After taking prescribed antibiotics for diseases and infections, the good bacteria and fungi in our bodies are depleted. That is why it's a great idea to rebuild that flora as soon as possible by supplementing with probiotics for a few days to a week. The same is true with soil. The use of insecticides, fungicides, and herbicides kills everything, all the good and all the bad microorganisms.

If compost is the pill form of probiotics, then compost tea is the intravenous form. It is more powerful, stronger, and faster acting, and less goes a long way. It should only be applied twice a year when the weather is just right in the fall and spring. If it's too hot or cold, the microbes will die before they have a chance to build the soil, roots, and external cellular structure.

Compost tea reduces the amount of water needed, releases locked-up nutrients in the soil (which decreases the amount of fertilizer needed), and creates an environment that weeds are adverse to by increasing the fungal content. This is obvious in nature when you walk through a forest with high fungal soil—there are very few weeds present. It breaks up soil, which allows better drainage, builds the immune system of plants to make them fight off viruses on their own, decreases soil-borne pathogens, builds a rich soil structure, protects foliage from airborne pathogens, breaks down heavy metals, balances the soil's PH, prevents blossom end rot, regulates soil temperatures that will also regulate plant temperatures, and builds a healthier, stronger, and larger root system.

Before there were synthetic chemicals, compost and compost tea were used for fertilizer. American Indian tribes buried the bones of fish in the soil where they grew vegetables. When making compost tea, fish emulsion is used to feed the mycorrhizae fungi. Using the fish bones also adds calcium to the soil. A lack of calcium is the cause of blossom end rot in vegetables. As agriculture grew in the United States, farmers used compost tea. It's not a new concept. We used it when we had a closer relationship to the land and what it could provide for our families and communities. However, the concept was lost when mass production became the focal point for agriculture. Adding synthetic chemicals helped eliminate pests and weeds, reduce fungi, and boost crop production.

I went through a similar situation in my life. As a younger person I was more likely to seek holistic ways of treating all ailments. As I aged into motherhood and was much more tired, I relied on Western medicine for a quick fix. Now, as a more mature version of myself, I have gone back to natural practices and save the manmade chemicals for only desperate measures. Are we as a whole nation going to be reverting to a more natural harmonious way of practicing agriculture? The practical use and science behind beneficial microbes has developed to the point where people are beginning to not only trust it but are also using it rather than synthetic inputs and saving the manmade chemicals for when nothing else works.

A proper tea consists of high-grade compost. The best kind of compost is homemade; however, if that is not possible at the moment, Nature's Way 50/50 is an excellent alternative. When making tea and distributing it, use only plastic utensils and buckets. Compost tea naturally breaks down heavy metals and will naturally destroy any metal used within a short period of time. The night before brewing, steep a few handfuls of your compost in a 5-gallon bucket using non-chlorinated (water without chloramine, which is how city water is treated), two tablespoons of fish emulsion, and two tablespoons of liquid seaweed. These two ingredients feed the fungi and bacteria, respectively.

The next morning, transfer steeped compost into a cloth teabag (search for compost tea bags online), pour tea steeped with the teabag in a larger container (I use a 64-quart bucket). Begin moving the water with an air pump. Oxygen needs to be added to the water to build the microbes. All the water should stay in constant motion. Add a few tablespoons of humic and fulvic acid with blackstrap molasses (or food grade molasses without salt). Place the brewer in an area outside where it receives zero direct sun and there is good air flow. If the temperatures are cooler, it will take longer for the tea to brew. In warmer weather, the brewing time takes as little as twenty-four hours. It's the smell that tells you if you did it right. It should smell earthy with a hint of sweetness. There should be no bad smell to it at all. Until the tea is ready with its sweet nature fragrance, it will smell like dirty old socks.

Another excellent sign your tea is ready is the thick layer of froth, which should be at least 2 inches thick. The thicker the froth the better. The more I researched the tea and brewing, the more I began to doubt I was doing it right. But that was only my mind trying to make me doubt myself. Making compost tea, just like anything else (soap, canned goods, fermented foods, a garden design) is so easy once you take overthinking and too much research out of the equation. Trust your nose and trust your instincts.

Once the tea is brewed, apply it to everything as a soil drench, a foliar spray, or both. Applying it first thing in the morning while the morning dew is still gently coating the foliage of plants and after the soil has been well watered is the absolute best time for the microbes to work their magic. The microbes use water as transportation to get where they need to be. It is important to dilute your tea with either rainwater or non-treated well water at a rate of 10:1—ten parts tea to one part water. A little goes a long way. As a foliar spray, gently cover the tops and underparts of the leaves. As a drench, only about a fourth of a cup is needed per plant. Of course, the larger the plant, the more you will use. An established tree will need to be treated around the outer edges of its canopy rather than at the base of its trunk.

Use all the tea within 72 hours of brewing. When finished with the application and brewing, the most important part of the process begins: the cleaning. Cleanliness is essential. Any leftover fungi or bacteria could create a harmful tea the next time. Use Dawn dish soap and scrub every item used in the process of brewing—the steeping buckets, tea bag, brewing container, pump and hoses, and the items used for application like the sprayer and the watering can.

The garden center I worked at would buy $10,000 worth of bareroot roses annually that we would pot up and grow ourselves. Growing roses in our subtropical zone is very tricky. They are incredibly susceptible to fungi, root rot, and thrips that would get in the buds and force them to drop without ever opening. The company invested large amounts of money on extremely toxic fungicides that we applied once every two weeks to protect from a crop loss. We also applied systemic insecticide that lasted an entire year to kill thrips before they damaged the buds. When I finally began brewing a healthy compost tea (it didn't happen the first few attempts, but persistence paid off), I applied it to our roses, and within twenty-four hours, the black spots were gone, new growth began to appear, and buds formed within two weeks. The tea worked overnight. For one year we only used the compost tea on the newly established plants, once in the spring and once in the fall.

For the home garden, I use it once in the fall for one to two weeks after planting new shrubs or trees to give the root system a boost of energy, and once in the spring. Living in this area of the country, microbes grow and multiply quickly. We are in the Arctic jungle, after all.

The first few times of brewing tea, I noticed changes in me. I was brewing on a large scale at the garden center and made new batches every two weeks in the spring and fall. The physical changes I noticed were stronger, healthier fingernails. I'm not sure if the clarity I began to experience was strictly from the tea or from the bowl-cleansing effects after using my bare hands to stir and transfer from the steeping bucket to the brewing contraption. Whatever it was, I was cleaned out, thought clearly, and had more energy. As an experienced tea brewer, I highly recommend using rubber gloves in the entire process. There's no need to overdose on microbes.

Earth's Antidepressants

My children's pediatrician asked me the first time we met if my children played outside and if they did it barefoot. The answer was yes, and my pediatrician gave a giant nod of approval. They are barefoot more often than I am. Scientific research shows a significant amount of health benefits from practicing "earthing" or "grounding," which is walking barefoot. Living in an area with weather conducive to outdoor activities year round is certainly a perk to living here.

Walking barefoot builds your immune system by allowing the microbes from the soil to enter the body through the skin, increasing the gut microbiome. Because of the earth's uneven topography, pressure points on the feet are naturally pressed. Walking barefoot decreases inflammation, lowers blood pressure, improves heart health, and improves sleep. Allowing our feet to touch the earth not only calms our soul but our bodies have a biochemical reaction to it, which then calms our minds.

The earth produces negative ions that release dopamine and serotonin in our brains. Dopamine and serotonin are the molecules responsible for our happiness. Dopamine gives us an instant sense of pleasure while serotonin creates a long-lasting feeling of happiness and well-being. Negative ions are heaviest near or in large bodies of moving water such as oceans, rivers, waterfalls, heavy rainstorms, and dense forests, particularly pine forests.

While negative ions increase our well-being, positive ions deplete the amount of negative ions we store in our bodies. Positive ions make us feel depressed, anxious, and stressed. Electronic devices, fluorescent lighting, synthetic material, and air pollution create the most positive ions. Our bodies absorb these just by being near them. Our bodies have a biochemical reaction to them. This is the world we live in, and escaping it is not possible. However, just one experience in an area dense with negative ions can produce enough serotonin to last for months. For more information on this read *Your Brain on Nature: The Science of Nature's Influence on Your Health, Happiness, and Vitality* by Eva M. Selhub and Alan C. Logan.

My husband's family has an acre of property along the Colorado River. My initial reaction was to be grossed out. I come from an area where the rivers are clear, you can see fish swimming, and the water is ice-cold glacier water. Here, the waters are warm and brown, and the visibility is nonexistent; however, for the most part, the floor of the river is sandy with only a few shells, unlike the giant slippery river rocks I'm used to. It's a pleasant treat for the feet. The view from the river is dense, jungle-like, and extremely Southern, like taking a ride back in time on the Mississippi River in Mark Twain's *Huckleberry Finn.*

Every time we fish on the river, I see at least one bald eagle. There is so much life—wild muscadines, dewberries, snakes of all kinds, giant catfish, alligator gars, deer, racoons, armadillos, owls, and vast amounts of horsetail reed growing along the banks. Horsetail reed is a hollow grass with a single bloom on top. It contains the highest amount of silica compared to any other plant. Silica is the primary element involved in the repair and formation of cartilage, bone, skin, and connective tissue. The spring shoots with fresh cone-like blooms contain the highest level of silica. I use fresh horsetail reed in my compost tea during the steeping process and also make a regular drinking tea with it.

The Colorado River and my husband have a special soul connection. He has told me over and over again that he goes there to feel happy. Every time we get to the river, the air feels heavy, rich, and earthy. The body relaxes and moves more slowly. I have been a firsthand witness to many people coming to the river for the first time and their sudden slowness, sitting around doing nothing, smiling, and soaking it all in. The first time I went to the river, I too felt the density of the air, the lushness of the grass (which never gets fertilized), and the majesty and soothing sounds of the sycamore and cottonwood trees when they shake from the slightest breeze. We walk around barefoot the entire time, all the way down to the sandbar. My husband Will taught me how to enjoy the water—finding something firm to grab onto, usually making deep holes in the sand for his hands, and hanging on and letting his whole body relax underwater with the river flowing over his entire body while minnows kissed all over his skin. It's an experience that stimulates all the senses. Then there is the outdoor shower that only covers the mid-section of the body on all four sides, exposing the feet, calves, shoulders, neck, and head. It works by connecting the water hose to a pipe that attaches to a shower head. Being so close to nature makes everyone a better person.

I've always loved the smells and sounds of the forest. Something triggers inside my brain that words can't describe. It's like my mind lets go of everything. The colors, smells, and sounds of nature fill my soul while my mind lets go. The colors of the few thriving wildflowers and foliage of plants are vivid and stand out brightly in the shade of the forest. The smell of decaying trees attracts me. Growing up in the dense forests of Teton County, Wyoming, I have chewed the sweet juices out of freshly decaying trees.

My daycare would take us on full-day hiking trips in the summer, about two a year. We hiked in the valleys of mountains and always inevitably ended up at a body of water. The water was always freezing cold fresh glacier water, but that never stopped us from playing in it all day. As a young girl, I can still recall the smells of the wilderness and colors of the wildflowers, the way the sun lit up the open fields, and the darker, deeper colors of the shadowy forests. When the sun peaked through an open spot, the colors were vibrant.

My parents took us on very long, tumultuous hikes. On those hikes, I was just trying to survive and couldn't pay attention to the sights. The only times on our hikes where we slowed down and were still was when my mom found a medicinal plant. "That flower is a cinquefoil. You can eat the leaves. That is yarrow. Apply that to wounds when you get them. Yarrow stops the bleeding, numbs the sore, and works as a natural antiseptic." I chewed on anything I could. To distract my mind from the intensely long hikes with my family, I searched for anything I could eat or put in my mouth—wild strawberries, huckleberries, the tender part of grass when you pull the long stem with the flower (culm) from the old growth (node). Some are sweeter and more supple than others. I always liked to do comparisons and find the sweetest type of grass. Then there was the wild honeysuckle that grows like a perennial weed and is bright red. And if I found the perfect piece of freshly decomposing tree—chow time!

My soul needs the natural environment to survive. I am not whole without that connection of nature to my heart. That is exactly how I feel in my gardens. I need to dwell near a city because of work. We need money to live the lives we live. But I have created and am continuing to create a wild, natural environment at my house. My parents and friends say they feel close to nature when they come to my house. Knowing I can give the people I love that feeling warms the cockles of my heart. Gardening is food for my soul.

Water Is the Source of Life

Nothing can live without water. No landscape is complete without it. The sound of running water naturally calms the mind. That's why it's used in many meditation practices. Without water our pollinators and natural predators wouldn't survive. It's pertinent to have both running water and still water near your garden. Bees, butterflies, birds, and bugs all need water to live. Most insects will only drink from still water (birdbaths, dew, puddles), but birds are attracted to running water. They still drink from still water, but running water from a fountain attracts them to a yard, along with trees, of course. Plants and microbes also need water.

Many areas are supplied with treated water from the city. That water became very rare during winter storm Uri in 2021. Pipes were freezing, causing extreme water damage in our poorly insulated houses. Our treatment facilities were no exception to the freezing temperatures. In Houston's surrounding areas there was a boil water alert. We saw people getting dyed water from fountains and retention ponds to use in their homes (hopefully they weren't drinking it).

It is pure chaos when there is not enough drinking water available.

Water companies use either chlorine or chloramine in the water supply to kill disease-causing germs. The chlorine or chloramine also kills the beneficial microbes in our guts and in our soil. That is why when using treated water, we replenish the beneficial microbes back into the soil by using compost, compost tea, or humates. We also need to replenish those lost microbes back into our guts.

Living in the country allows for access to well water. The well water in Southeast Texas is full of minerals and heavy metals. This is good and bad. It's great for watering outdoor plants but bad for the house due to all the calcium, magnesium, and iron that destroy appliances, leave scale on showers, and stain everything, including the foliage of plants to a rusty yellow color. When I first moved to an area with well water, every houseplant or fresh cut flowers I watered with it either died or came close to death. It took me a few weeks to figure out that it was the minerals and metals that were causing the issue. We have a water softener that alleviates the damage caused by the rich minerals to our house, but it also adds sodium, which kills plants. Plan number one to healthy indoor plants, people, and pets was to install a reverse osmosis (RO) water system to purify the water. RO makes water as close to distilled as possible by removing all the sodium and any other minerals and metals. It also filters out glyphosate and nitrates caused by industrial agriculture, which has potentially leached into the well water since we live in the middle of row cropping agriculture. House plants perform best with RO, distilled, or treated water from the city.

Plants outside thrive with mineral-rich well water; however, the softened water from the house will kill them quickly. Make sure the water softener only goes to the interior faucets and keep the regular well water to the exterior faucets. We had to install new water lines directly from our well to reduce the amount of death we were seeing in our gardens. Our septic system also releases softened water, so the plants getting watered by that are at risk of death.

For most of my time living in Texas I watered by hand. This is best if you have the time to do it. It is one my favorite parts of gardening and allows me to wake up with the sunrise outside and listen to the world wake up. First it's the birds, and then it's human life and insects. Watch the sky go from dark to pink and purple with a warm glow of orange and gold, to a light blue with soft yellow tones. Listen to and watch the soil and plants soak in the life-giving water. It is the perfect time of day—quiet and alone with your thoughts except for all the life starting to stir in your presence. It is also my favorite time to write. There is always hope in the morning to make a day one of the best days I've ever had in my life. Make today count. You get another chance to exist and make a difference or make things a little better. It is meditation.

Watering in the morning is best unless you see plants struggling in the evening. Then, of course, water the struggling plants. A morning drench is best because it allows the moisture on the leaves time to dry, an important step living here. Wet foliage leaves the plants more susceptible to fungi, which grow rapidly at night. Like the lawn, it is best to do deep waterings a couple times during the week rather than every day for a short period of time. Deep watering causes the roots of plants to search for water deeper in the soil, giving them a stronger chance for survival by lessening the plant's dependence on the gardener. In gardening, watering is the most important part to learn and the hardest part to master. Overwatering kills a plant faster than underwatering by causing root rot. It's best to water at the roots in the soil, but when it's triple-digit temperatures, plants enjoy getting their foliage wet. Plants, like humans, perspire. But plants will perspire through their foliage. Touching the leaves of orchids or other plants is a fun experience. You can feel their temperatures, and when it's hot, the foliage will feel extremely hot. After watering them, the leaves will cool to a normal temperature.

I collect rainwater, but like all things, I could do it better. We started with just 5-gallon buckets placed under our spouts, but now we have large tanks for storage. Rainwater is magical water. It is naturally soft water without the salt and is slightly acidic, which is fabulous for our alkaline soils. Jorge, a friend of mine, saw our small collection of rainwater and asked what I did with it. He told me that back in Mexico, his mother washed all their white clothes in the rainwater, which left them brighter and softer than any washing machine or detergent could do. My oldest daughter has figured out on her own that she can naturally whiten and brighten her white Crocs by washing them with rainwater.

Plants know when a storm is coming, and soon a slow plant dance commences. Squash plants make the biggest performance as they lift their large leaves upright to allow for more water penetration into the soil where their roots are. Also, the shape of plant foliage channels the water to exactly where the plant wants the water to go. It's a fascinating, slow-moving, botanic rain dance.

There are certain areas in my yard that capture and hold more water than other areas. These areas are for building a rain garden. Rain gardens are low areas that have poor drainage during the rainy season or storms but are dry during periods of drought. Planting the right plants helps cure the drainage problem while adding a special area to the yard. The areas that hold the most water in my yard are under and around my oak trees. I've noticed that oaks have their own special way of surviving. It's as if they suck soil down, creating low spots beneath them to capture and hold water for their deep root system. Plants for rain gardens are as follows:

- *Crinum Lily:* There are several varieties of these you can choose from. Some varieties grow in ditches and bloom in spring (my husband has named them ditch lilies). Other varieties are more spectacular with intense colors and fragrance. During a mild winter they will be an evergreen; in cold or freezing winters they will defoliate. Some varieties are small, and others will grow 6 feet tall and wide. Sun is required for blooming.

- *Mexican River Spider Lily:* Also related to the crinum and amaryllis, these bloom for several weeks in the spring and in the early summer have beautiful white blooms. They enjoy wet soils along rivers and waterbeds.
- *Lycoris:* These are also known as the surprise lily. They bloom in the late summer to early fall when nothing else will. Lycoris radiata is the variety that performs best in my area.
- *Turks Cap:* This is a Texas native that takes full sun or mostly shade, but they look thirsty during droughts and in intense heat. Hummingbirds love these special perennials that bloom nearly year round.
- *Canna:* This is a gorgeous tropical perennial that thrives in our weather—flooding, freezing, drought, heat, and humidity. Cannas gently spread, and once they are planted, a commitment has been made.
- *Wax Myrtle:* These are not very pretty, but they are mighty. The bark, berries, and leaves of this large shrub have many uses. It has a woodsy herbal fragrance, which makes the leaves an ideal substitute for bay leaves in soups and stews. The bark can

be harvested in the fall, dried and smashed into a powder later to be used internally or externally to treat sore throats, ulcers, itchy skin, and dandruff. Internally it is used to treat bowel issues, colds, and flus. It increases circulation, keeps bacterial infections at bay, and assists with excessive menstruation. Do not use if you are pregnant. The wax from the berries can be used to make aromatic candles and any other use you can think of for wax.

- *Iris:* These are excellent for boggy areas. Louisiana iris love our heat and humidity.
- *Wildflowers:* Planting native wildflowers such as coreopsis, bluebonnets, and Indian paintbrush on the outer edges of the rain garden adds a darling touch of beautiful wild nature.
- *Pink Muhly Grass:* This is also known as Gulf muhly grass. It is a perfect addition to the rain garden. It can handle drought and massive rain, doesn't spread, and is gorgeous in full bloom in late summer through fall.
- *Gingers:* There are many varieties of gingers. Shell ginger (alpina var.) is excellent for part sun to mostly sun. Butterfly ginger (hedychium coronarium) is incredibly fragrant. The rhizomes are edible and medicinal (just like the kind you buy at

> the store but a milder flavor), and they grow wonderfully in the shade. Shampoo ginger's (zingiber zerumbet) rhizomes are medicinal and edible, and like its name, you can make shampoo out of the juices from the blooms. These grow best in filtered sun to part shade. Curcumas thrive in full sun to part shade with showstopping blooms.

There are many plants suitable for rain gardens. These are just a few. We have the perfect soil for rain gardens. The clay soil has a very slow percolation rate, which prevents water from draining too fast. Rain gardens need to be in an area with poor drainage in full sun at least 10 feet from the house.

Irrigation has been one of the best investments I have made. Drip irrigation is ideal for flower beds. Even with irrigation, I still need to water at least once a week. Before irrigation, I was watering my flower beds and gardens by hand for a total of eight hours a week. With irrigation, I have condensed my hand watering to about two hours or less per week, which is remarkable during a summer drought.

Having a water schedule is important. Plants have memories and minds. Everyone has heard that your plants do better when you talk to them; they also do better when you touch them gently while pruning with clippers or scissors rather than tearing. And wow, do they perform if you give them consistent water so they don't have to guess if they need to stop performing to conserve energy for survival.

Watering teaches you to slow down, be present, observe in silence, and not exert too much energy. Just be still in the moment. It's rare for me to just stop doing and be still and patient. Watering forces that on me.

Drought-Tolerant Gardens

The truest thing about living in Texas is that you cannot predict weather or its patterns. But I receive great joy trying to predict what the weather is going to be like. Everyone has their own little system of making their own predictions. "Every ten years we have a three-year drought." "If we have a hurricane, we will have a cold winter and snow." My favorite is this one: "If we have an ugly winter, we will have a beautiful spring." For the past three years, we have had bare minimum and below bare minimum rainfall. Even though we have long periods of extremely dry weather, it is vital to plant the drought-loving plants in an area that does not hold water. There are several plants that enjoy this.

- *Texas Mountain Laurel:* This is a must-have, extremely slow-growing ornamental tree. The blooms in spring are fragrant, almost like the smell of grape jelly, and it's a host plant to the broom moth caterpillar, an important source of food for birds and lizards. Butterflies and bees love the spring blooms as well.

- *Reblooming Bearded Iris:* This one is gorgeous and fragrant. It blooms in spring and periodically through the summer after a good rain and in the fall. It enjoys poor soil but needs some shade in the afternoon during the summer.
- *Vitex:* Also known as chaste tree, this is a fast-growing large shrub that can be trimmed to look like an ornamental tree. It blooms from spring through fall and has medicinal benefits for women's health as well. The berries are used to assist in relieving premenstrual syndrome (PMS), infertility, and menopausal issues. For men, the berries decrease sexual drive, hence the name *chaste*.
- *Hamelia Patens:* This is also called hummingbird bush or fire bush. It grows 7 feet tall and 5 feet wide. It's a perennial, so it will die back every winter and slowly come back in the spring to be a full-grown shrub, continuously blooming from summer until the first frost. Hummingbirds cannot resist this plant.
- *Yucca:* This is a personal favorite of mine and reminds me of Wyoming. Cows in Wyoming wrap their giant tongues around the blooming stems and lick off every bloom. The long fibers from the leaves have been used for everything—string, dental floss,

rope, and more. All species of yucca are edible. The blooms can be eaten as well as the fruit. The roots are medicinal and can also be used as a shampoo.

- *Agave:* Like yucca, all parts of the agave plant are edible and can be used in the same way. We would not have tequila without this gorgeous plant. Because it is a succulent, it needs no fertilization, fungicide, or pesticide, making it the most organic form of alcohol.
- *Prickly Pear Cactus:* This is a beautiful plant whose fruits are extremely high in vitamin C and other antioxidants. It protects against many diseases and lowers blood sugar levels. Make tea or preserves, or eat it cooked or raw. The leaves or paddles are used in Mexican dishes with eggs, salads, tacos, and soups.
- *Caesalpinia Pulcherrima:* Otherwise known as pride of Barbados, it is an excellent-performing perennial that is freeze-tolerant. It blooms from summer until frost with giant show-stopping blooms adding tropical color and texture.
- *Oregano:* It is an amazing herb that grows into a beautiful, rounded, blooming 2-foot-tall and wide evergreen perennial. To keep the plant from losing its potent medicinal properties, remove the blooms when they appear. Oregano is also medicinal and edible. It repels pests and is frost tolerant.

- *Purslane or Portulaca:* It withstands the driest of conditions and is an excellent low-growing annual for summer color.
- *Asiatic Jasmine:* In particular, snow-n-summer Asiatic jasmine. It's gently mounding, gently spreading, and easy to maintain. Thriving in part sun to mostly shade, it changes colors to white the more sun it gets; hence the "snow" in its name. It makes for a fabulous ground cover in shadier gardens.
- *Boxwood:* This is an excellent evergreen shrub that requires little water once established (after three years), but it gets burned in severe freezes.
- *Holly:* All holly varieties are wonderful performers for our area. My favorite is yaupon holly, a Texas native. The berries are poisonous but make for an excellent fresh-cut centerpiece during the holidays.

Bringing Nature Indoors

As a working mother who possesses the innate desire to care for all living and nonliving things, it only made sense to have plants indoors. My first plant ever given to me was in college when I was nineteen. It was a banana plant. I had seen it alone in an empty room and quickly moved it to my dorm room. When the owner (a very handsome young man with an affinity for plants) discovered I had moved it to my room, he kindly allowed me to own it forever. After moving from my sunny dorm room to a less well-lit apartment, I struggled to keep the banana plant alive. I tried my absolute best. I brought it into the bathroom with me every time I showered.

The second plant ever given to me was when I was twenty. It died twenty-three years later and traveled around the country with me. A gorgeous Easter cactus was given to me by Camille, an art major friend of mine. She had just graduated from college, was moving out of Wyoming to San Francisco, and gifted me the beautiful plant. She told me it never bloomed, but for me, it bloomed every year.

I kept it indoors throughout my years of traveling and living in different places. It survived Texas, which speaks volumes for its strength. You have to be strong to live here because everything tries to kill you, from the insects carrying deadly viruses to the ants with their poisonous bites to the stinging grass and the chiggers. Even the pollen will try to kill you. I have managed to save two beautiful cuttings from the mother plant, which will last the rest of my life and my children's lives. I would love it if they passed cuttings on to their children and their children's children.

The Easter cactus is a reminder of my friend Camille. She was so talented and inspired me in every way to delve into my own creativity. Camille offered me two plants. She said she could never get them to bloom. After two years, they bloomed heavily for me. I gave one away because of all the traveling I was doing, not knowing where I was going to live or for how long I was going to be there. The other stayed with me through everything, the longest relationship I have had other than the relationships with my parents and sister. The trick is, they need to be root-bound, which means their roots need to feel tight in their container in order to bloom. Also, it's important not to feed them. It's a waste of money. They gain their nutrition from the air. If you want to give them a little extra nutrition, like all other cacti and succulents, adding a layer of earthworm castings to the top of the soil is the best way to fertilize.

Plants clean the toxins out of the air and increase productivity, concentration, and creativity. They reduce stress and are therapeutic. They add life. When I walk into a house with houseplants, I get a feeling of nurturing and safety. It's a different kind of energy like seeing someone's heart on display. They're exposed and working quietly and patiently to do their job. They don't require much of anything, just consistent watering. I remember as a child my mom made me clean her plants in the house. In a bowl she mixed one tablespoon of milk with one cup of water. The calcium in the milk prevents tip-burn, and wiping off the dust allows for better photosynthesis. I would gently wipe each individual leaf with the concoction, leaving the leaves shiny, healthy, and clean. I have my children do this chore now. It is calming and rewarding. Plants react when they are cared for. They stand taller and put on new growth. Some will bloom.

Proper soil and watering are the two scientific methods to ensure successful houseplants. Drainage is essential, so use planters with holes in the bottom to allow the water to escape. Using reverse osmosis water, rainwater, or distilled water instead of soft water is important. Soft water will kill your plants within a very short period of time. Indoor plants are susceptible to root rot, a condition that occurs when the soil retains too much water and never gets the opportunity to dry out between periods of watering, causing a bad fungus to destroy the root system. Fungus gnats, which are tiny little flying black insects, are attracted to fungus in the soil. They lay their eggs in the soil, and their larvae, once hatched, feed on the fungus.

Using a high-quality soil helps with drainage to build a

healthy root system and has the ability to dry out between watering. There used to be only one product to buy—Miracle-Gro potting soil, which is one of the worst soils I have ever used for houseplants and for potting plants outdoors. Fox Farms Ocean Forest is the best soil I have found for container growing both indoors and outdoors, but I'm sure there are other soils coming out on the market that will be ideal for this as well. Fox Farms Ocean Forest contains beneficial microbes that help prevent soil-born fungus, along with bat guano and earthworm castings (worm poop). When looking for a high-quality soil, find ingredients such as good microbes (bacteria and mycorrhizal fungi) that fight off bad fungi. Allowing the soil to completely dry out between waterings will assist in the prevention of bad fungi and the gnats they attract.

A very good friend of mine always told me she had a black thumb and couldn't grow anything. Everyone says that when they try and fail with their first few plants. What makes someone great with plants is caring for them, giving them energy, and paying attention to their needs. Does it do better with more light? Is it drooping and the soil is really dry, which means it needs water? Or is it drooping and the soil is moist, which means it has too much water? Touching and paying attention to the plants tell them you care for their survival. Care and energy are essential to all growth. Babies who are never held or talked to will develop at a much slower rate and tend to be smaller. The same is true with plants and all life.

Having houseplants in the South is different from having them in Wyoming. Texas has more humidity naturally occurring in the winter and is drier in the summer due to running the air conditioner almost constantly. Through thirteen years of trial and error, I have narrowed them down to a few of my favorites.

Indoor-Loving Plants

- *Pedilanthus:* It grows upright with variegated foliage that turns pink to red the more sun it receives.
- *Christmas and Easter Cactus:* It receives much of its moisture from the air and is easy to propagate. It blooms from Thanksgiving to Easter, depending on the variety. The blooms evolved over time to become more appealing and easier for hummingbirds to access.
- *Philodendron Ivy and Pathos:* All varieties perform well, even in low light. They are easy to propagate and become a fuller plant when cut back on occasion. They are incredibly quick-growing.
- *Spider Plant (Chlorophytum comosum):* This plant handles neglect very well and creates many little babies you can grow new plants from.
- *Dracaena:* All varieties are fabulous and perform well in lower light areas. The more light they receive, however, the more colorful they become.

- *Peace Lily (Spathiphyllum):* It enjoys being dried out between watering and can handle low light conditions. Its blooms are white and will bloom more frequently the more light it receives.
- *String of Hearts (Ceropegia):* It's trailing and delicate. I love everything heart-shaped because love is the most important thing in the world.
- *Aloe Vera:* This is an essential. The plant performs much better outdoors, but it will do well indoors provided it has bright light and dry soil. It is also the most powerful of all house plants, cleaning the air of toxins. It encourages positive energy while filtering out negative energy.
- *Stephanotis:* It loves bright light and will need its roots to be root-bound (grown tightly together) in order to bloom. It's the symbol of marital happiness and encourages a healthy sex life.
- *African Violet:* This is an all-time classic indoor plant. These soft blooming plants remind me of grandmothers. The more light they receive the more they will bloom year-round.
- *Ponytail Palm:* It loves bright light and needs very little care or water.
- *Burros Tail:* It grows best in southern-facing windows with bright light and little water.

- *Bird's Nest Fern:* This is the only fern that performs well indoors. As an epiphyte, it captures moisture out of the air, making it an ideal plant for humid, well-lit rooms such as the kitchen or bathroom.

- *Hoya:* This is a plant that reminds me of a grandmother's house. It aids in spiritual enlightenment, strengthening our alignment with the divine. Every variety will bloom a little waxy bouquet of flowers with a delicate fragrance.

- *Rubber Plant:* This plant is uniquely easy and large. Do not overwater it. It symbolizes abundance, happiness, and resilience.

Growing plants indoors is an excellent first step for those plant lovers who have a very limited amount of time to care for much else but still want to reap the benefits of having clean air and a calm mind. Here are five things to remember when growing houseplants:

1. Invest in proper soil that provides good drainage and has the ability to dry completely. Every few years use compost as a top dressing 1/4 inch thick, which rejuvenates the soil.

2. Water only when necessary. Do not use softened water. Use distilled, reverse osmosis, or rain water.

3. Provide bright light.

4. Wipe off foliage with a combination of water and milk to help prevent tip burn and open the cells for better photosynthesis.
5. Fertilize with earthworm castings.

The Herb Garden

When COVID began, the world became chaotic. I turned off the television and never turned it back on. There were shortages of everything, from tissue paper to ibuprofen. The news was full of fear. That fear jumbled the thoughts in my mind to the point that I had trouble thinking clearly or logically. One thing I did know was that there has to be an alternative to waiting for a synthetic cure. One day I woke up and thought, *What do I have planted around my house that I can use just in case?* And that is when the research began on the medicinal properties of everything growing around me.

It's the natural progression of coming into your own as a gardener, to begin indoors and bring the inspiration outdoors. Entertaining friends and family has always been something that brings me joy. Using fresh herbs in the dishes I prepare is important to me. Even if it is more in my head than reality, the food tastes better. My guests would agree, but I'm not sure if it's because I mention which home-grown organic herbs are used in each dish. And herbs are the easiest things to grow.

Because of herbs, I am able to make my own salad dressings, herb-encrusted fish, turkey, prime rib, tenderloins, sauces, teas, floral arrangements, gift decorations, luxurious baths, and the list goes on. Not only is the flavor enhanced, but herbs provide medicinal benefits as well.

My husband and I took a romantic vacation to Costa Rica. It turns out that I am prone to motion sickness, and after a full day of vomiting as a passenger in a car from our location near the volcanos to the beaches on the western coast, I thought there was no hope for me. Our vacation was surely ruined. We arrived at Villa Caletas and were greeted with ice-cold wet face towels steeped in lemon verbena. The fragrance immediately soothed my upset stomach. My mind and body released all pent-up stress instantly. Since that experience, my heart has been drawn to lemon verbena.

Herbs were the first thing I planted that made me feel like a successful gardener. They also made me feel like a successful gift-giver. Giving gifts is not my strong suit. I have friends who make me feel special due to the thoughtful gifts they give me. Unfortunately, I am not like that. But I have discovered my gift in gift-giving, and it includes herbs. I love the creativity of wrapping presents with paper or cloth and making a bow with herbs and flowers. The decoration of the wrapped gift is much more spectacular than the actual gift; it is also much more enjoyable than shopping for the gift. Making the card with a drawing or painting on the front and handwriting something in it gives my friends and loved ones a little part of my heart. It may not cost much, but it is priceless and one-of-a-kind.

For me, the herb garden brings joy, peace, and a feeling of independence. When there is a cut, I go to the garden or have the kids go to the garden to pick leaves of yarrow. I wet it down and apply it to the wound. It not only numbs the area in question but stops the bleeding and works as a natural antiseptic without killing any cells. My mother taught me about yarrow when I was five or even younger. It grows wildly where I come from in Wyoming. My father, on the other hand, was a fervent believer in iodine. No matter what the wound, my father's first response was iodine. He would walk around with blotches of deep yellow on random parts of his body—hands, fingers, knees, arms. "You have a broken arm? Let's put a little iodine on it. That'll do the trick. You have spaghetti sauce on your white shirt? Use some Windex." Windex and iodine would cure any issue. A few years ago, my dad stopped using iodine because he learned it not only kills bad cells but also kills good cells. And cells don't repair themselves as quickly as we age.

There are bacteria living in our well water. Most people aren't affected by it; however, I am. When the intense summer sun comes in contact with clothes washed without borax, the bacteria releases a strong fragrance I call "sun." I'm not particularly fond of its distinct fragrance. My scalp is also sensitive to the bacteria. When it heats up, it itches, but using a strong rosemary tea after a shower instantly soothes my scalp and takes away the itch and inflammation.

Rosemary Tea

- 2 cups distilled or reverse osmosis water
- Several sprigs of rosemary (the more the better)
- 2-quart saucepan with lid

Put all ingredients into the pot and bring it to a boil, allowing it to boil for three minutes. Cover and turn off heat, letting it cool completely.

Remove the rosemary and transfer the liquid to a dark glass spray bottle and store it in the refrigerator.

Spray it on your scalp after every shower to relieve itching with its anti-inflammatory properties. It also increases the shine and subdues frizz. You can also spray it on cuts or bruises.

The best time to harvest herbs is in the morning after the dew has dried and the oil content is at its highest levels. I used to dry herbs using a dehydrator set on the lowest heat. This is wonderful if you are only using herbs for flavoring. When dehydrating, there are still some medicinal components in the herbs, but even at a low heat it is too fast for the oils to be fully and adequately released. Nature dictates how and when to release the medicinal properties in the form of oil. Using a heating process for drying can have detrimental effects on natural antioxidants in herbs. For medicinal purposes, fresh herbs have lower levels of beneficial healing qualities, and herbs that are dried using heat also have less medicinal properties. The process of water evaporating through drying causes the walls of the cells of the plant holding the oils to rupture, releasing the essential oils. Allow plants to dry naturally. Hanging them upside down in a room with air flow and sun makes the natural process of drying occur, which releases the oils at just the right pace. Drying flowers is best done on a loosely woven basket or an old screen so the air is able to flow through. You should dry roots the same way you dry flowers, in loosely woven baskets in a well-ventilated room with ample sun.

When combining herbs for teas, stick with relaxation herbs mixed with other relaxation herbs such as lavender, lemon balm, holy basil, valerian root (a little goes a long way as it is very potent), and borage. The same is true for stimulating herbs such as roselle hibiscus, rosemary, and echinacea.

Throughout history, or at least recorded history, herbs have been relied upon for healing in every culture. The Bible talks of herbs and plants. Every church or castle I've ever visited has an herb garden for medicinal purposes, not just culinary. During my years in college, I was weirdly drawn to monasticism. I grew up going to a First Baptist church because it was the most attended in our little community in Jackson Hole. My father was determined to be successful with his own business in a small town, and part of becoming a respected member of a community was to attend community functions such as church.

It was a very good church, a large cabin-like building made of dark brown painted logs and huge stained-glass windows at the altar. I enjoyed dressing in pretty dresses for church, but sitting still for an hour through the sermon was painful. My mom would pinch me if I made too much noise or squirmed too much. So I took to drawing miles and miles of looping roads on the service card.

I attended summer Bible camp a couple of years until I was old enough—ten—to assist with the infants one year. I loved that. Being with the babies was the best part of church. Going to church ended in our family when my parents decided to divorce. But church remained a pure part of my life. While my parents were divorcing and focusing on themselves, I was galivanting about town with my newfound freedom (or so I thought it was freedom), spending my time with my friend Kelly who lived in town within walking distance to everything. Her home life was also tumultuous, so we spent as little time in her house as possible. It was my idea to go to the church, whose doors were always open. We would go to the pulpit, turn on the microphone and sing and sing and sing. We tried to play the organ but would get caught and kicked out of the church. Even though we didn't attend very often, church felt like a kind and loving home to me.

My mother was raised Irish Catholic. She didn't bring that religion into our home except for the guilt aspect. She was the master of shame and guilt. I always assumed this was a Catholic thing. But it didn't stop me from being fascinated with Catholicism and even more so the devout monks and nuns who committed their lives to service for God.

In college I took every religion class available. I wanted to be a nun, to have that deep, personal relationship with God. But the thing is, I already had that deep relationship; I just didn't know how to activate it. There is an abbey near Wyoming's border in Colorado. After passing the sign several times on my way to Fort Collins, I finally decided to stop in one day for a look-see. It was quiet. I had the place to myself except for a couple of nuns I saw working in the garden, or maybe I didn't see them. I do remember the garden and flowers and the calm, peaceful life. I walked into the church and was greeted by a running fountain of holy water that I touched with my finger and made the sign of the cross like I had seen before. Sitting in one of the pews all alone and facing the altar, I was in search of a sign or a voice from God. I sat for what felt like a very short moment in time when, coming from nowhere, I heard sweet angelic voices singing. I looked around without seeing any other person in the church and just assumed the singing was coming from angels. So I continued to sit. The songs didn't stop. I stood up to leave, and that's when I saw nuns high above in the church singing. It was magical and serene. It was a romantic lifestyle, but not one made for me.

When I completed college and traveled around the United States, I went to visit my friend Summer in Germany where her husband was stationed. We drank beer, listened to music, and visited darling rustic towns where we immersed ourselves in German culture. There were parades, music, and festivals everywhere. People dressed in lederhosen and dirndls were playing and dancing to polkas, and it wasn't even October yet. We explored castles and churches. Each castle had its own elaborate church. The two aspects of each castle or monastery we visited that pulled at my heart strings were the herb gardens and the kitchens. There is a comforting feeling that emits from herb gardens, like a holy spirit is present. This was the medicine provided for everyone in the community, the source of healing. Each kitchen, even though they were no longer in use, felt like the beating heart of the castle. The energy from all the creating and nourishing was palpable in each and every kitchen.

The kitchen is the heart of every house. It's where people gather, open their hearts and souls, and share their dreams. Herbs heal. I love seeing in my kitchen windowsill the freshly cut herbs in jars of water waiting to be utilized, bringing the garden inside.

The flavor comparison between fresh and store-bought are so far from each other it's hard to believe you have purchased the correct herb. Harvesting herbs once or twice a year when they look their best and then drying and chopping them in a food processor for use throughout the year is so simple, and the flavor is more powerful than store-bought dried herbs.

In the window by my desk I keep a clipping of rosemary in a jar. I rub the foliage between my fingers, releasing the fragrant oils. Breathing them in deeply stimulates my mind and memory. Rosemary is also one of my most preferred herbs to include in the bows of wrapped gifts I give to my friends and family. We are just beginning to discover the power of aroma and its effects on the brain and body.

When company comes to town, I always make a very tiny bouquet composed of flowers mixed with lavender. The goal is to have my company sleep so peacefully so sleep becomes the healer and they remember their visit to my house as being relaxing. I also enjoy making tea for my guests in the evening to induce sleep.

Calming Sleep Tea (aids in sleep)

- Holy basil
- Lemon balm
- Mint
- Sage
- Chamomile

ImmuniTea (fights off viruses)

- Roselle hibiscus
- Sage
- Oregano
- Holy basil

Women's Tea (balances hormones)

- Roselle hibiscus
- Mint
- Mugwort

Combine equal parts of each herb. Steep 1 teaspoon for 5–10 minutes, and enjoy.

Chamomile is possible to grow here, but it doesn't produce very much and quickly dies from the intense heat and humidity. It can be found growing wildly in many other parts of the country like Wyoming, flowering and ready for harvest in July through August. There is a different effect, a stronger purer effect on the mind and body from fresh tea.

Growing herbs made me feel like a successful gardener. They are easy, require little maintenance (no need for fertilizers), and provide comfort knowing you're growing your own natural pharmacy available to you at all times. Herbs are also the source of much of my creativity. I absolutely love adding them to homemade soaps. Holy basil adds color and fragrance to soap, not to mention the cell-rebuilding properties it possesses.

It fascinates me that in every culture, in every religion, and in every moment in time herbs have been used for healing. What perplexes me is how each culture discovered the healing properties. Did God whisper to them in a dream?

Herb	Container/ Bed	Require-ments	Benefits	Uses
Basil, African Blue	Bed, near or in vegetable garden	Dry soil full sun. Annual.	Attracts beneficial insects, leaves are high in vitamins A & C & K, boosting the immune system and healing wounds.	Flowers: garnish cocktails and in teas Leaves: best used in Middle Eastern dishes, used in tea, & topically for healing wounds.
Basil, Holy (Tulsi)	Bed, front entrance of the house or sacred space	Dry soil full sun. Reseeding annual.	Same as African Blue Basil but also the following: protects organs and tissue, stress reducer, balances blood sugar, blood pressure and lipid levels. Reduces psychological stress, improves memory and cognitive function. Balances mind, body, and spirit.	Flowers: garnish cocktails and in teas Leaves: best used in tea, & topically for healing wounds. Use fresh leaves in cooked dishes, baths and soap. Dried flowers and leaves best used as a tincture or in capsule form. The fragrance itself is therapeutic.

Herb	Container/ Bed	Require- ments	Benefits	Uses
Basil, Sweet	Bed, near or in vegetable garden	Dry soil full sun. Annual.	Same as African Blue Basil but also the following: reduces stress and memory loss, supports cardiovascular health, boosts digestion and detoxifies the body.	Fresh leaves and flowers in teas and cocktails. Leaves fresh or cooked or dried in all types of cooking, most com- monly used in Italian & Mediterra- nean dishes and in salad dressing.
Bay Leaf	Raised beds with well drained soil and protec- tion from freezes	Dry soil full sun to part shade. Tender evergreen shrub or small tree.	Aids in digestive tract function, calms urinary tract and den- tal infections. Used to calm inflammation in joints.	Fresh leaves are used in cooking stews, soups and sauces. Infused in oil to use topically.

Herb	Container/ Bed	Require-ments	Benefits	Uses
Bergamot Bee Balm, Monarda	Beds near the garden	Rich, well draining soil in mostly sun with some shade	Relieves coughs, eases cramping, induces calm, relieves urinary tract infections, reduces fevers, general relaxant	Use fresh or dried foliage and flowers. Best if used as a tea at night. Can be used in honey and tinctures and as a steam inhalation.
Borage	Beds, near or in vegetable garden	Full sun. Reseeding annual.	Attracts beneficial insects for natural pest control in the garden. Calms the nervous system aiding in relief from stress, exhaustion and grief	Use fresh flowers and leaves in salads and cocktails. Use dried flowers and leaves in tinctures and teas.
Chives	Beds or container in the garden	Dry soil full sun Semi-evergreen perennial	Improves soil, attracts beneficial insects and deters pests. Improves memory functions while improving bone, cardiovascular and digestive health.	Use fresh in every dish, with hot dishes add at the last moment to ensure maximum flavor. Use in salad dressing and marinades. Dry and use later.

Herb	Container/ Bed	Require- ments	Benefits	Uses
Comfrey AKA: Ass Ear	Beds, tropical gardens	Full sun to full shade. Moist soils. Perennial	Attracts beneficial insects. Reduces inflammation and assists in the growth of new skin cells healing cuts and bruises. By sucking up all the nutrients and minerals through its roots, the foliage makes a natural fertilizer fantastic for compost piles.	DO NOT CONSUME. For wounds, bruises, sprains and joint inflammation, only use topically, in a bath or soaked leaves as a compress on problem areas for 20 minutes. Cut leaves go directly in gardens or in compost piles to provide a natural N-P-K.

Herb	Container/ Bed	Require- ments	Benefits	Uses
Dill	Beds near the garden but not in the garden.	Full sun to part shade. Well drained soil. Reseeding annual	Attracts beneficial insects. Host plant to Black and Anise Swallowtail butterflies. Assists diges- tion, improves immune func- tion and bone growth. Used to treat colic and helps with breastfeeding.	Both seeds and foliage can be used in many dishes such as cucum- ber salads, soups, breads, roasted potatoes and dips. Also fre- quently used in pickling. The seeds and foliage can be used fresh or dried.
Echinacea	Tropical gardens, raised beds.	Full to part sun, rich, moist, well- drained soil. Perennial.	Attracts ben- eficial insects. Treats fatigue and skin conditions. Boosts the immune sys- tem and helps build white blood cells. Helps increase fertility.	Leaves, flowers, and roots are all used dry or fresh in teas. Roots contain the highest content of medicine and should only be harvested in the second year.

Herb	Container/ Bed	Require- ments	Benefits	Uses
Fennel	Beds near the garden but not in the garden. Plant away from Dill to avoid cross pollination.	Full sun to part shade. Well drained soil. Reseeding annual.	Attracts beneficial insects. Host plant to Black and Anise Swallowtail butterflies. Assists diges- tion, balances hormones, antiviral. Curbs appe- tite, increases breastmilk production.	Seeds, foliage, and bulb can all be consumed fresh. Seeds fresh or dried are used after a meal to freshen breath and aid in diges- tion. Bulb can be added to soups and salad. Foliage is used in cocktails. Commonly used in Italian and Indian dishes.

Herb	Container/ Bed	Require- ments	Benefits	Uses
Hibiscus, Roselle	Raised beds.	Full sun, in moist well-drained soil. Annual. Plant seeds in March.	Attracts beneficial insects and hummingbirds. High levels of antioxidants, naturally stimulates the mind and body, builds strong bones and teeth, and suppresses appetite. Cleanses the liver and helps manage diabetes and high blood pressure.	Use fresh, dried, or frozen calyces. Remove seed pod inside before using. Let a few seed pods dry on the plant to save seeds for planting in spring. Use in hot and cold drinks, as a jam, in smoothies. Use fresh blooms, calyces and leaves in salads.
Lavender: Fern Leaf, Spanish, Sweet, English	Beds or large containers	Partial sun in rich well-drained soil.	Reduces anxiety, stress, blood pressure, depression. Relieves insomnia. Reduces symptoms of PMS and hot flashes.	Best used as an essential oil, however having fresh cut lavender by your bed is just as effective. Use dried flowers in teas, desserts, soaps and baked goods.

Herb	Container/ Bed	Require-ments	Benefits	Uses
Lemon Balm	Raised beds.	Full shade to part shade. Well drained soil. Perennial.	Promotes sleep, reduces stress and anxiety, soothes the heart and assists in better sleep.	Use fresh or dried leaves in teas or sauces, salads, marinades, tinctures, water or cocktails, and as an essential oil.
Lemon Grass	Containers or raised beds,	Full sun to part shade. Well drained dry soil.	Promotes sleep, relieves pain and inflammation, reduces stress and lifts mood. Immune builder.	Use fresh stalks, chopped and mashed in mortar and pestle. Add to marinades, meat, ice-cream, curries, and sauces. Use fresh leaves in tea, baths, soups and slow rested meats. Fresh bruised stalks are used in cocktails and waters.

Herb	Container/ Bed	Require- ments	Benefits	Uses
Marjoram, Sweet	Raised beds, or Containers.	Full to part sun. Well drained soil. Tender annual.	Aides in digestion, heals gastric ulcers, and menstruation. Strengthens the nervous system reliev- ing stress and anxiety. Reduces cough and clears sinuses.	A cousin to oregano with a more del- icate flavor. Use fresh or dried in sauces, salad dressing, marinades, salads, soups, on poultry, in teas or fresh leaves in essential oils.
Mexican Mint Marigold	Raised beds.	Full sun to part shade. Drought and heat tolerant. Perennial.	Attracts beneficial insects. Heals digestive issues. Used in ceremonies in Mexico and ancient Aztec traditions. Repels worms and increases stamina.	Petals and leaves are best used fresh. They do not retain their flavor when dried. Use in salads, soups, and teas.

Herb	Container/ Bed	Require- ments	Benefits	Uses
Mint	Containers only.	Full to part sun. Well drained, rich, moist soil. Hardy trailing peren- nial. Will become invasive.	Attracts ben- eficial insects and deters pests. Aids in digestion and heals respira- tory issues. Helps balance hormones.	Fresh leaves are used in teas, cooking, marinades, and cock- tails. Fresh- ens breath. Essential oils can be added to showers for a luxuriously refreshing experience. Orange mint is the easiest to grow.
Mug wort	Raised beds.	Full sun to part shade. Well drained, rich, moist soil.	Antifungal, antibacterial. Aides in digestion, balances hormones, reduces high blood pres- sure, boosts energy and calms nerves.	Flowers and foliage are used dried or fresh in teas, in baths, as incense and made into bitters.

Herb	Container/ Bed	Require-ments	Benefits	Uses
Nastur-tium	Raised beds, or containers and in or near vegetable gardens.	Full sun to part shade. Reseeding perennial.	Repels insects, attracts beneficial insects. High in minerals and vitamin C, antibac-terial and antifungal.	Leaves, stems and flowers are all edible. Make a tea out of leaves to treat coughs and colds, use in gardens as a trap crop. Garnish salads and appetizers with fresh flowers.
Oregano	Raised beds.	Full to part sun in well drained soil.	Reduces infec-tions, aids in digestion, improves bone health, treats the common cold, improves heart health, detoxifies the body, and attracts bene-ficial insects.	Use fresh or dried leaves and flowers. A staple in Mediterra-nean and Italian dishes. Use in salad dressing, marinades, or herb encrusted meats. Use dried for healing teas and tinctures.

Herb	Container/ Bed	Require- ments	Benefits	Uses
Parsley	Raised beds or containers.	Full to part sun in well drained soil. Butterfly gardens. Hardy biennial.	Host plant to Black Swallowtail butterfly. Cleanses kidneys and aids in digestion. Rebuilds cells in eyes protecting vision. Lowers blood sugar and contains flavonoids which protect against cancer.	Use fresh or dried leaves and stems as a garnish to everything. Add to salad dressing or fresh sprigs to smoothies. A wonderful addition to almost every dish.

Herb	Container/ Bed	Require-ments	Benefits	Uses
Rosemary	Raised beds or containers. Near vegetable gardens	Full sun to part shade, well-drained dry soils. Hardy perennial.	Rich in antioxidants, anti-inflammatory, boosts the immune system, improves blood circulation. Stimulates your brain improving memory and performance. Improves hair and scalp quality, and supports the digestive track.	Use fresh or dried in marinades, salad dressing, to potatoes, on fish, beef, poultry, pork, or lamb. Cut a sprig to keep at the desk in a glass jar to reap its aromatic benefits. Make an essential oil for hair and skin.

Herb	Container/ Bed	Require- ments	Benefits	Uses
Sage	Raised beds or large containers.	Full sun to part shade. Drought and heat tolerant. Perennial.	Rich in antioxidants, anti-inflam- matory. Treats digestive, circula- tory, upper respiratory, and mem- ory issues. Relieves depression and excessive sweating. Quickens the senses and delays age associated cognitive decline.	Known as the healing herb, use dried leaves and flowers to make tinctures. Use dried or fresh in all types of cooking, salad dress- ing, eggs, fish and poultry. Dried and burned it can be used to purify the air of bacteria.
Savory, Winter	Raised beds or large containers.	Morning sun and afternoon shade. Well drained rich soil.	Assists with prevent- ing early orgasm and calming sex drive. Calms digestive issues such as cramps, indigestion, diarrhea, gas and nausea.	Delicious; used as a rub or marinade on meats. In salad dress- ings, finely chopped with eggs, or whole in beans.

Herb	Container/ Bed	Require- ments	Benefits	Uses
Thyme, Mother Of	Raised beds.	Full sun to full shade. Makes a sweet ground-cover. Perennial.	Strong anti-septic, antioxidant, anti-inflam-matory and assists in balancing the nervous sys-tem. Resolves respiratory issues.	Fresh or dried leaves used in teas, and cooking. Essential oil is used in agriculture as a fun-gicide and insecticide.
Valerian Root	Well-drained raised beds with rich compost.	Morn-ing sun to part shade, rear of the herb garden	Relaxes and calms the nervous sys-tem and mus-cles. Relieves tension, stress, and anxiety (should not be used with other anti-depressants). Assists in deep sleep.	Dried roots are used for teas and baths. Fresh roots are used for tinctures and baths. Harvest roots after year two.

Herb	Container/ Bed	Require-ments	Benefits	Uses
Verbena, Lemon	Well-drained raised beds with rich compost or containers.	Full sun to part shade.	Treats bronchitis, insomnia, anxiety, digestive and heart issues. It has also been used to decrease tumor sizes.	Use leaves fresh or dried; use as a substitute for lemon in dishes. Make essential oil, sachets, tea and add to baths for a relaxing soak. Great for marinades.

The Annual Garden

I've tried to have gardens without annuals, but they aren't the same. Annuals add all the instant gratification of color needed to show a property is loved and tended to. Of course, it's not just about aesthetics because that would be too superficial. They provide so much more—pollination, beneficial insects, natural healing properties, natural protection against root knot nematodes that are detrimental to plants, and nitrogen-fixing (natural fertilizer) properties.

An entire bed does not need to be covered by annual flowers. Little pockets of color add much more visual interest. Annuals here are not exactly annuals. I have dianthus still blooming and spreading from five years ago. I've had several other plants reseed themselves, including snapdragons, marigolds, calendula, zinnia, viola, gomphrena, vinca, larkspur, and celosia. Others have come back from the roots or bulbs, such as salvia, dianthus, pentas, coleus, petunias, and caladiums.

Annuals are essential. They make everything seem better taken care of than they actually are. Looking out my windows

I can lose track of time staring at them. I like to take my family on nature identification walks throughout the seasons to show them what new plant is growing and what new blooms are appearing. There is always something new happening in the gardens.

The blooms or foliage of annuals are showier than anything else in the garden, and just seeing the different colors brings me intense joy. Next to herbs they are the second-easiest plant to grow. Most annuals I plant from pots are already established, but there are some annuals that do so well grown from seed that it makes more sense to plant them that way. When planting an already established plant, dig a hole, add diatomaceous earth and compost, gently massage the roots, plant them, cover the top with a thin layer (1/4 inch) of compost, and then leave them alone. Fertilizer will not be necessary until later in the growing season. Plants are grown with fertilizer at greenhouses. There is no need to continue adding it.

Growing from seed is a little more difficult. The problem we have with this is mainly caused by ants. I like to say that Texas is just one giant ant hill. Ants will eat the seeds I have purposefully planted, which is very frustrating. Rarely will any flowers from seed packets I receive at weddings or in gift baskets (primarily wildflower and pollinator varieties) actually germinate and produce. There are some seeds I have better luck with than others such as nasturtium and zinnia. It wasn't until the fall of 2024 when I discovered that using diatomaceous earth as a soil amendment has the ability to protect seeds from ants and many other small insects.

Growing up in the mountains of Wyoming, I was taught at a very young age how to eat ants in a survival situation. The ants I grew up with were large and scarce. Down here, if you don't pay attention to where you are stepping in nature or your yard, before you know it you have fifty ants biting you and trying to take you down. I moved to Texas as an adult, and my first experience with ants was painful. It took me weeks to heal from their bites. Both my girls' first experience with ants happened when they were less than a year old as they were crawling in the grass. In their cases, just ten to fifteen bites caused them to have a fever. After the initial experience, our bodies built up a tolerance to their bites. We can now heal in just a few days after being bitten. It's fascinating how our bodies naturally build up tolerance to all things in order to survive. Plants, animals, the earth, and humans are all alike in that way. As my experience has grown and through observations I've made, I don't hate ants as much as I used to.

The areas where ants have made their home tend to have the best soil. It's light and fluffy with excellent aeration. I've seen ants pulverize cockroaches and assist in decomposition better than anything else out there. In the extreme heat of the summer or the freezing cold of winter when the bees seem to hibernate or migrate, the ants take over pollination. They are pains in my ass when I'm pulling weeds or planting seeds, but what I have noticed is that the more I work in the bed and disturb the soil, the less tolerance ants have and will move out. When I see an ant mound in my soil, I disturb it, and, slowly but surely they all move to a new home. Once they do that, the soil is fabulous and the absolute best for growing plants. I noticed it at the garden center I used to work at as well. The pots with the nicest looking plants usually had an ant colony living in them. An excellent remedy for ants in pots is drenching the pot using a gallon bucket of soapy (Dawn dish soap) water. It kills the ants through suffocation and leaves behind rich soil. Bulbs are an excellent way to get the joy from planting a seed without sacrificing it to ant colonies.

> Sometimes when you're in a dark place
> you think you've been buried,
> But actually you've been planted.
> —Christine Caine[1]

Bulbs remind us that when we think we are drowning in life's situations, we are actually growing. It's hard times that teach us character, build our confidence, and bond relationships, ultimately making us better people. After planting bulbs, you sit back and slowly watch the emergence of

---

[1] Christine Caine (@ChristineCaine), "Sometimes when you're in a dark place you think you've been buried, but you've actually been planted," *X*, August 2023, https://x.com/ChristineCaine/status/1690752319275905024.

life from deep in the soil. There is something so magnificent when we witness such a giant—beautiful life emerging from a small bulb. I interpret it as a sign from God. There is hope that life will continue—and not just continue but adapt to survive, that everything we need to survive is already inside us. Tulips in particular are magnificent, the first things to emerge from hibernation after everything has been bitten by the random winter freeze and the garden is sparce, brown, and bare naked. Once the blooms finally emerge, they begin the day tightly closed, and as it warms up, they fully open like a majestic poppy and then close again for the evening. It's almost as if the flowers are breathing with the day.

Caladiums have the same impact. As the summer heats up and the flowers start struggling to stay full, slowly thinning out and dying back, giant lush foliage begins emerging from deep in the soil, making the garden fresh. Seeing bulbs like caladiums thrive in heat and humidity triggers in my brain that the weather is not as hot as it actually is, because if it were, no plants would survive. The large foliage also works as an umbrella to protect the soil from the intense heat and rays of the sun.

Planting an already established plant like those in a 4-inch, quart-size, or gallon pot is generally the way I go. When I do receive some flowers from seed, it brings me tremendous joy, and I consider it a gift from God who made every living thing on purpose for a reason. All of life is a constant change. Nothing is set in stone, and we must be willing to try new things because that is how we grow.

Caring for annuals, no matter what time of year, is the same. If there is a tool to make life easier, I will use it. When I was seven years old, I broke my elbow on the growth plate from jumping on a trampoline playing Break the Egg with my older sister and her best friend. The two girls were twice my size, and as I was sitting cross-legged holding tightly to my feet, they double bounced me at the same time. I flew a mile into the air and saw the whole world under me. As I made my descent, I extended my right arm behind me to brace for the fall. My forearm bent backward, snapping my elbow. After the operation, the doctor told my parents there was a strong possibility that my arm may not grow any larger than it was at seven because of the location and severity of the break. I'm grateful my parents never shared that information with me as a child of seven.

Just like in Lulu Wang's story (the movie *The Farewell* based on her real-life events), the whole family kept the secret of their grandmother's stage 4 lung cancer from the grandmother who was diagnosed. She was given three months to live. However, because the grandmother didn't know she was dying, she ended up living several years longer than expected. Her story left such an impression on me. I truly believe our minds are so incredibly powerful and what we stress will happen, will happen. Stress, worry, anger, or any other negative feelings do not allow our bodies to heal.

My family kept from me the secret of the potential for my arm not being able to grow, but I did heal and my arm grew normally. As an adult, I can only use my right arm so much before it begins aching with inflammation that lasts for the next seven days, limiting any activities I have planned. But there is a tool that transformed how much I can plant and how quickly. Before the tool, I could only plant two or three flats (thirty-six 4-inch pots) of color. After the tool, it's unlimited. That tool is the Power Planter, an auger with a hex bit used with a drill. It changed the way I plant. It easily breaks through fibrous roots while aerating the soil and making the plants develop their root system more quickly than using a traditional method with a hand trowel or shovel. I even use it to turn the soil in my raised beds.

I discovered another life-changing tool just recently. In August 2024 I met an eighty-five-year-old man from India named Jagan. He introduced me to his products MegaSilica and AgriDiatomSil. The first product is diatomaceous earth in granular form, and the second is amorphous diatomaceous earth in powder form. I have used DE for years, mixing it with chicken feed to kill parasites, feeding it to my cats and dog, and using it to kill ants, including crazy ants. I've even consumed it. It's important when purchasing diatomaceous earth to make sure it is amorphous rather than cylindrical, which is not safe for animal or human consumption and is carcinogenic.

Jagan was put into my life at just the right time. I had just finished a conversation with my friend, a farmer, who had discovered that very summer that he could no longer use insecticides because they caused a desperate allergic reaction, causing his eyes to swell shut for a couple weeks at a time. Fifteen minutes after hearing the news from my friend, Jagan appeared with an alternative approach to industrial insecticide in agriculture. Use diatomaceous earth with a little non-ionic surfactant (Dawn dish soap helps the DE stick to the surface of the plant) diluted in water as an insecticidal spray. It not only works but also has many other relevant benefits.

My intrigue was ignited. Why has something so natural and beneficial not been common practice all along? That fall, I implemented DE in my gardening practice with everything I planted, using it as a soil amendment. Amorphous, food grade, OMRI (Organic Material Review Institute) diatomaceous earth is not only effective in killing eggs, insects, parasites, snails, and pill bugs, but it also has many benefits. DE decreases the uptake of toxic elements and heavy metals by attracting and trapping the positively charged toxins to their naturally negatively charged surface area, thus rendering the toxins and metals unavailable for cellular uptake. Diatomaceous earth increases available phosphorus, which encourages early root development, heat, drought, and salinity tolerance. It absorbs and releases available water in soil and directly delivers it to the roots, making water wetter. DE is derived from fossilized diatoms, which are algae and small crustaceans. They are the beneficial compound silicon dioxide (SiO2), a naturally occurring mineral—silica—that is necessary in the overall health of soil, roots, plants, animals, and humans.

The results I discovered from my fall planting was inspirational and worth sharing. Black beans have become one of my favorite fall vegetables, but the plant itself is very weak, and if the wind blows, which happens all the time, the plant bends and breaks. After using DE as a soil amendment when planting the black beans by seed, I noticed incredible root growth early on, which caused me to thin the plants earlier than usual. When I pulled the babies up, the large root system was undeniable at a very early stage. For the first time since my journey with black beans, I did not have to stake up any plants. The structure and strength were noticeably improved. The stems and foliage were thicker and stronger with a more vibrant and deeper color. And the flower production had increased, which increased the fruit. The flavor was excellent. I decreased the amount of water and had increases in the beneficial bacteria and mycorrhizal fungi in the soil. When planting the rest of my garden, I noticed larger heads of cauliflower and a heavy production of broccoli. It could have just been the year, but I'm not willing to not use DE in all my planting from here on out. Although I still noticed white flies, aphids, cabbage worms, and flea beetles, there was no damage to any of my plants, and I did not need to spray anything.

When planting annuals, the first step is to place the plants in their desired spots. Once the spacing looks good, use the drill and auger to make the holes. Add compost to each hole. That further assists with enriching the soil and creating better drainage while also adding beneficial microbes directly to the roots of the plants. Then add DE about 3 tablespoons worth. Gently massage the roots of the plants, encouraging the roots to loosen so they can begin their process of growing larger and stronger in the flower bed. Once I have finished planting, I mulch, keeping the mulch far enough away (about 2 inches) from the base of the plant. Mulch and compost have the ability to decompose, especially with freshly planted items. Water everything well. Then keep an eye on watering. The most common destroyer of plants is too much water—overloving if you will. Just because I'm hot and thirsty does not mean my plants are too.

After a period of either extreme heat or extreme cold, all plants will benefit from a light cutting back and an additional gentle spreading of fertilizer or compost. This encourages new blooms and new growth.

Spring and Summer Annuals (there are more, but these are my favorites)

- *Angelonia:* This is a heat- and sun-loving annual but will live much longer in mild winters. It's deer- and rabbit-resistant and an excellent pollinator with a slight tender fragrance. The flowers symbolize love, affection, and purity, and are often used in weddings to symbolize the love between two people.
- *Caladium:* This plant is not for human consumption. It loves heat, humidity, and water. It does

well in full shade, full sun, or in between. Also known as the Heart of Jesus, the caladium symbolizes divine love for humanity, a selfless love overflowing with compassion. Just looking at the foliage brings calm and relief from stress. The bulb can be planted anytime between mid-April and mid-August. It is the easiest summer annual to grow with the most vibrant color. Plant in August for amazing fall color that will last until the first frost. Keep it planted with good mulch during the winter, and it will return for the next few years.

- *Celosia (Cock's Comb):* This plant loves heat, humidity, and drought. It is originally from India, grown as a crop planted in full sun to part shade. Plant from April to May for color lasting through the summer and well into the fall. The vibrant colors look like a Spanish painter decided to liven up the garden. Leaves, tender stems, and young blooms are all edible and packed full of vitamins. Medicinally it's used to treat gonorrhea and jaundice, and is a powerful antioxidant when the seeds are made into a tincture. Celosia will reseed itself year after year.
- *Coleus:* This can be planted in full sun and full shade. It's one of my favorite true annuals. Each plant will grow the size of a shrub, adding

interesting color and texture to the summer garden. Plant in June for color lasting until the first frost. Remove the blooms to continue sending energy to the growth of the foliage. Or leave the blooms on and let them go to seed for free plants the next year.

- *Gomphrena:* My heart has always been drawn to gomphrena for reasons I do not know completely. They are so incredibly easy to grow in drought, heat, and full sun. They reseed themselves, coming back year after year. The blooms never stop throughout the summer and well into the fall. Butterflies and bees swarm them. The blooms make long-lasting fresh cut and dried flowers. When made into a tincture, the leaves are used as a detoxifying herb that purifies the blood due to its potent antioxidants and richness of vitamins and minerals. Plant from March through June en masse for an exceptional display of sweetness in the garden.
- *Impatiens:* This plant is excellent for shady, damp gardens, but it is susceptible to fungus, in particular powdery mildew. One way to help prevent this is the use of compost tea on the foliage in the spring (one application is all that is needed). Another way to prevent the fungus is to use compost as mulch, which will form a protective barrier

between the soil and the plant. They are the only annual flowers that will truly shine in a shady garden. The bright colors of the blooms bring a sense of calm and tranquility.

- *Melampodium:* The plant is deer-resistant, drought-resistant, and heat-and-humidity-resistant. Butterflies, bees, and other pollinators are attracted to the darling blooms, and in fall, the birds enjoy the seeds. Do not remove the plant from the garden and watch it come back from the roots in the following years. Plant in full sun to part shade.

- *Penta:* Grown best in full sun to part shade in well-drained damp areas, pentas come back by the roots. So, if the plants are well mulched, you can expect to enjoy them year after year. Butterflies and hummingbirds find them irresistible, particularly the purple-lavender color. To really draw attention to the beds, lipstick pink color does not disappoint.

- *Peppers (Ornamental):* Recent studies show that these peppers are excellent for planting with roses to help control thrips (an insect that damages flower buds and foliage buds) by acting as a banker plant (a plant housing the predatory mite that eats up to twenty thrips a day). The Black Pearl ornamental pepper is an outstanding performer in containers and in the landscape, taking well to the heat and humidity.

- *Torenia (Wishbone Flower):* This plant does excellent in full sun to full shade and has the potential to reseed itself. Research has shown that the edible flower possesses powerful antioxidative ability. The flower from Torenia is a symbol of wishes coming true.
- *Verbena:* Plant this in full sun—at least eight to ten hours a day—to experience its magnificent blooming power. Butterflies love these heat-and-humidity-tolerant annuals. Homestead purple is excellent as a border of intense color and will last two years.
- *Vinca (Periwinkle):* An absolute favorite heat-loving, drought-tolerant plant, it can be planted in full sun to part shade and will reseed if the conditions are right. The delicate annual is susceptible to blight caused by a fungus living in the soil. Planting it in June or later is one way to avoid the fungus. Using a thin lay of compost as mulch around each plant creates a barrier between the soil which harbors the fungus and the plant which is damaged by the fungus.

Fall and Winter Annuals

- *Alyssum:* This is the most popular cool season annual. They attract beneficial insects and repel rabbits from gardens. It is an interesting topic in the garden because of the fragrance. When I was pregnant, it smelled like dirty gym socks and stinky jock straps. As my hormones balanced back to normal, the fragrance was like a sweet perfume. Alyssum is edible, a darling addition to cocktails, salads, and desserts.
- *Calendula:* This is an absolute must-have for sunny, well-drained areas. Planting in gardens in the fall helps bring pollinators and traps aphids. The blooms are edible and full of medicinal oil. I dry the blooms and make calendula oil by filling an airtight jar with the dried blooms and covering them with a high-grade olive oil. Leave the jar in a cool, dark place, and shake it every day. After six weeks, I use this oil for salads, face serums, and ointments. Calendula flowers, fresh or dried, have the ability to repair cells. I use fresh petals in salads and as a garnish. Dried flowers can be used as a delicious floral tea that repairs internal cells. Or use the dried flowers with dried roses to make the most soothing and repairing astringent.
- *Cosmos:* I struggle with these flowers, but that doesn't stop me from planting them every year

in the fall. I plant them because they remind me of growing up in the mountains with butterflies swarming them. When I see the blooms, my mind is transported to a garden that exists only in my dreams. It's worth it. While they do last, they provide ample amounts of fresh-cut flowers that last several weeks in a vase. If I do get lucky with a particular variety, I harvest the seeds to replant them in the fall.

- *Delphinium:* These are show-stopping! Plant them in November by transplant. There is no need to protect them in freezes. They do excellent in full sun and almost full shade. The blooms are huge in the spring, making them perfect for fresh-cut floral arrangements. I had these planted in the front of my house when we put it up for sale, and I'm sure that is what sold the house right away. They were the only thing blooming in a dreary February.
- *Dianthus Chinensis (Mounding; Floral Lace):* This is one of my most favorite low-growing, gently spreading annuals. Mine have lasted five years without covering during freezes in full sun and full shade. They do an excellent job protecting beds from erosion while attracting butterflies, bees, and other beneficial insects to the garden. It's deer-, rabbit-, chicken-, and drought-resistant. The whole plant has been used in traditional Chinese

medicine for its antioxidant, anti-inflammatory, antiviral, antibacterial, and antifungal properties.

- *Dianthus Barbatus (Upright; Amazon and Jolt):* This is an upright dianthus variety with larger, more vibrant blooms. These varieties do not last as long as the mounding variety and need protection from freezes. Plant in the fall and deadhead for continual blooming.
- *Foxglove (Digitalis):* This is a magnificent annual, best when planted in the fall. It takes all winter to develop its roots and foliage enough for a spectacular spring display of giant blooms reminiscent of an enchanted garden. Beneficial insects cannot resist the blooms. Historically and currently the plant is being used medicinally for congestive heart failure. However, the plant is also known to be deadly if ingested.
- *Hyacinths:* Plant this pre-chilled bulb in the ground, containers, indoor, or outdoor in mid-December through mid-January. Their delicately but distinctly fragrant blooms freshen the air indoors and outdoors. There's no need for protection from cold; they love our cold, wet winters. They are the first bulbs to bloom in February when other plants are still recouping from freezes.
- *Larkspur:* This is a species from the delphinium genus. This variety acts like a perennial, coming

back year after year through reseeding itself. Just like the delphinium, it is an excellent pollinator, show-stopper, and fresh-cut flower. The flower symbolizes an open heart, joy, and love. Do not ingest this plant because it is highly toxic; however, the flowers have been used as dyes and for making a topical tincture that is said to kill lice and other external parasites.

- *Lobelia (trailing):* This is a gorgeous, low-growing, gently spreading annual. Use as a fabulous border in partial shade to full sun. It is delicate but packs a punch when planted en masse, looking like a sea of sparkles. Plant in the fall and cover during a freeze, and by early spring watch the intense pop of its true blue color.
- *Marigold (Petite French Tangerine):* The best time to plant this incredibly necessary flower is in the fall. They may freeze back but generally will make it through either by seed or sometimes by the roots. This is a must-have in vegetable gardens and any other garden where root knot nematodes are present. Nematodes are attracted to the roots where they get trapped and are unable to continue their life cycle, or they can also be affected by the toxic chemical released by the roots when ingested by the parasite.

- *Nasturtium:* This is a wonderful trailing favorite for all types of gardens or containers. Planting by seed or transplant is ideal in the fall. They will freeze back but will generally come back quickly in the spring, or plant new ones in very early spring. The flowers are edible. I add a touch of cream cheese to the center of the flower or just use the flower for an edible decoration with my dishes. It has a slightly spicy flavor. The foliage is also edible, and both foliage and flowers can be used for tea to treat coughs or the common cold. Mixing the fresh foliage with lettuce, chickweed, spinach, and arugula for a salad or on avocado toast is heavenly.
- *Petunias (Bubble Gum Pink from Proven Winners):* This is by far the absolute best-performing petunia, with potential to last all summer. It looks wonderful in containers or the landscape. Petunias clean the air from pollution better than any other plant. They like dry conditions with full to part sun.
- *Poppies (Icelandic):* These are an absolute favorite of mine for full-sun gardens. I don't plant anything else with these. They stand out perfectly on their own with delicate, bright-colored flowers dancing above soft foliage all spring. They make excellent fresh-cut flowers that last two weeks in a vase.

- *Snapdragon:* This is a classic for cottage gardens, with the potential to reseed. They attract beneficial insects and hummingbirds to the garden. If deadheaded during the winter, the spring bloom is magnificent. Fresh-cut flower arrangements that include snapdragons have always been a favorite in Houston society circles.

- *Stock:* Fragrant and lovely, these grow best in part shade to full sun with well-drained soil. Like snapdragons, deadheading or cutting back lightly before spring promotes exceptional blooms. It is wonderful as a fresh-cut flower.

- *Sunflower:* Plant these by seed in mid-February and again in mid-August in a bed on the outer border of your vegetable garden. The giant blooms attract beneficial insects as well as harmful (such as leaf-footed stink bugs) and act as a trap crop (keeping bad bugs off good crops by attracting them). They also work as a perch and a food source for birds. I recently read that the spiny sunflower pollen may kill parasites living in bees' guts and increase the production of queen bees. Isn't that wonderful if it's true?

- *Tulips:* This is a breathtaking annual bulb. It's best planted 6 inches deep in full sun to full shade from mid-December to mid-January. There is no need to protect them from freezes. They are the first thing to bloom in spring, indicating hope for better days to come. Loving cold, wet winters makes this a no-brainer for our area. To ensure blooming, the bulbs must be chilled in a refrigerator for at least six weeks before planting or bought prechilled. They are wonderful for fresh-cut arrangements. Tulip petals with the stamen removed are edible. I have people get out of their cars and walk through my yard to my blooming tulips to see if they are real.

- *Viola:* This is the sweetest border plant with colorful edible flowers. Plant in the fall in full sun to part shade with well-drained soil. Viola prefer dry climates and soil, so with heavy winter rains, they are not nearly as beautiful as their full potential. Trim them back in mid-February for a spectacular spring bloom. Freeze fresh flowers in icecubes for a fancy cocktail addition. The blooms are edible.

Whenever I visit a friend, I pick a small bouquet of flowers, grasses, ferns, or whatever is currently growing around my yard, put them in one of my many recycled jars, and bring it to the visit. The reaction I receive always brings a smile and comfort to my heart. It's a simple, kind gesture that shows I am willing to do all the growing, and I will gladly share the rewards of my work. This is a tradition I also take with me when our family is camping in our camper. Using an old tequila bottle, we take a nature hike and fill it with a branch of a shrub or grasses in bloom. It becomes a welcome addition to our newest adventure.

The Perennial Garden

This is simply a list of the best perennials for our area. Care for perennials is just like annuals. The proper time to plant is in the fall—September through December. That allows the roots to become established over the winter for a hard-working spring and summer performance. Cut them back twice a year, once after a freeze with no chance of another freeze and once in August as the extreme heat begins to let up. After cutting them back, add a light dressing of compost and/or apply compost tea.

The perennial garden is the heartbeat of all gardens. Perennials have different blooming seasons. Providing each season with blooms allows for a robust natural habitat for insects and birds. At each house we lived in growing up in Wyoming, my mom planted Shasta daisies. She said she did it for me because I loved those pure white flowers with the cheery gold centers. They stand tall with their golden heart open for all to see. These were the flowers I would pick and remove petal by petal, beginning with "he loves me" and then "he loves me not, he loves me, he loves me not, he loves me, he loves me not" until I got to the very last petal—"He loves me!" Then I would pick another flower and do it all over again. For several minutes I was fully occupied. I didn't realize it at the time but what I was doing was a type of active mindfulness. I allowed my mind to not think but just have an action with my hands and some words to say, allowing my mind to clear itself and be calm. Just like praying the rosary or counting on mala beads.

My mom told me she planted the Shasta daisies because she knew they were my favorite flower. I want to believe that to be true. I never felt unconditional love from her, and as I have grown, it has become even less so. My mom is an addict. She was introduced to alcohol and drugs at a very young age. She was the product of the 1960s, sex, drugs, and rock and roll. I'm not sure when she began, but I believe it was in her early teens. Perhaps it was the drugs and alcohol that caused her to be emotionally stunted. It almost appears as though she never wanted to grow up, even when she was a mother and then a grandmother. My heart hurts for her at the same time it longs for her. As a mother, I realize that everything I say and do, my girls emulate. I am partially responsible for building their self-esteem. My mom had no self-esteem, and if my sister and I showed any, we were considered selfish. It was not tolerated to have any self-love. I did not grow up loving myself. It wasn't until I turned forty that I made it a goal to love and accept myself. I had to because I wanted my girls to grow up loving and accepting themselves.

I saw my mother being nurturing when she baked and gardened. I saw her nurturing when she sewed sundresses, aprons, bonnets, and curtains for us. I saw her nurturing when she nurtured her soul through creating and gardening. She taught me that. Gardening is healing as is bathing in the sun, soaking up the vitamin D, listening to the birds, seeing life all around, being in the moment, pulling weeds, thinking—there is a lot of thinking that goes on while gardening. With every bare piece of soil, I create in my mind what I would like to see, smell, touch, or eat, and that's what I will plant.

When I was sick, my mom made me some echinacea tea. Echinacea purpurea (purple coneflower) is one of my favorite perennials to grow here. The leaves, flowers, and roots are all healing. Using fresh or dried (dried is stronger medicine) leaves or flowers steeped in a hot tea is the perfect remedy for colds and flu. But the most potent part is in the roots. Harvesting roots after the second year of growth during the fall is ideal. Living in Texas, it's pertinent to have a dehydrator. Wipe off the soil from the roots and resist the urge to wash them. Allow the roots to dry in a well-ventilated sunny room, or dehydrate them on the lowest setting. Store them in an airtight jar in a dark, cool spot. Drink three to four cups daily to help fight off viruses. The echinacea flower is large, letting its heart lead the way as it points up toward the infinite sky. It will bloom from spring until the first freeze. I love its soft purple petals and rough cat-tongue-like foliage.

At a King Tut exhibit at the Museum of Natural History in Houston, I paid particular attention to the hieroglyphs. The lotus flower was present in many of the Ancient Egyptian artwork and played a major part in all of ancient Egyptian life. It was believed that out of the watery chaos in the beginning came a beautiful lotus blossom that opened up and released the sun. In some parts of the religion, the sun that emerged was Atum the sun god. Blue lotus flowers were later discovered in Tutankhamun's tomb, scattered on his body. The lotus flower is a symbol of the sun, creation, and rebirth, opening every morning and closing and submerging itself below the water every night. Not only was the flower prized for its intense fragrance, but it was also believed to have healing powers.

We suffered a severe drought and record temperatures in the summer of 2023. I went to one of the most beautiful botanic gardens in the south, Shangri La Botanical Gardens in Orange, Texas. Ruby Lake, a protected lake for several species of birds for breeding, was incredibly low. But I noticed something new about it. Protecting what little water was left from overheating and evaporating was a lotus flower I had never seen before. Nelumbo lutea (American lotus) with giant creamy yellow blooms is native to Texas. According to Jennifer, the Director of Horticulture at Shangri La Botanical Gardens, she had never seen the flower growing there before. It created shade on the water, protecting the fish population by cooling the water temperatures and allowing for good oxygen in the water and a perfect habitat for the fish.

Fish is the major food source for the migratory birds who have made birthing nests all around the lake. It's beautiful to think that nature instinctively reacts to adverse conditions to protect, heal, and persevere.

That is the miracle of perennials. They tell you what the weather is going to be like. In the winter, they stay dormant for longer if the weather is going to remain cold for longer. In the summer, they begin putting on new foliage at their base when they feel the weather will be cooling down soon. Living outdoors constantly allows them to become more in sync with the changes of time.

The first perennials coming to life in the garden after the winter are the bulbs—crinum lilies, American hybrid lilies, amaryllis, daffodils (narcissus), rain lilies, Mexican spider lilies, and Leucojum to name a few. That tells me spring is here. The lilies are not susceptible to diseases, fungus, or freezes, making them ideal as a northern-facing plant. Bulbs are also ideal for my gardens where the chickens roam. Our chickens dig up everything except the bulbs. I don't mind them going in and thinning out the insect population, but it does disturb me when they dig up freshly planted annuals. Even so, they do more good than harm, so I guess we'll keep them.

The American hybrid lily is a favorite. They begin emerging from dormancy in February, growing to 3 feet tall and blooming for six weeks beginning in May. I love these for the tropical garden. When they're done blooming, the foliage adds interesting texture to the garden.

Amaryllis are the first bulbs I bought when I moved to Texas. Sitting in the sun on a delicious fall day in November 2010 with boxes and boxes of amaryllis from Holland, Betty Lenderman (matriarch of Enchanted Gardens and Enchanted Forest) explained to me their splendor. We touched each 34–36 centimeter bulb with our own hands and gently pealed off the dark brown crispy outer layer to reveal a juicy pearly white with golden-brown and burnt orange accents bulb. We gently snipped the dried, dead roots and left the viable juicy roots. On each bulb we wrote the names of the cultivars. She explained that the size of the bulb was directly correlated to the age of the bulb. We were handling eight-year-old bulbs. It took eight years for each bulb to get to the size they were, which also meant that each of the six blooms per stock were giant. "You don't throw these bulbs away after they bloom," Betty explained. "You plant them in the ground with their shoulders showing above the soil in a well-drained raised bed with at least four hours of direct sunlight. Once they are finished blooming in the spring, cut the stock off in a diagonal direction 2 inches above the bulb to prevent water from going directly to the heart of the bulb and rotting it. Eventually, the large bulb planted will create pups, which you can cut off the mother with a few roots attached and share them with your friends. Some cultivars of amaryllis have lived here over eighty years."

The perennial narcissus (daffodils) for our area are Fortune, Carlton, Monal, Erlicheer, Ice King, Pipit, Avalanche, and Tete-a-Tete. Each of these come back year after year.

They are fragrant and a welcomed surprise. All daffodils are fragrant and make delightful fresh-cut arrangements that last two weeks. Daffodils are the flowers that mark the old homesteads all over the country. The daffodils I planted two years ago bloom at the beginning of March.

Perennials are wildflowers in my mind. Maybe that's why I love them so much. Even saying the word *wildflower* makes my mind wander to my childhood in the mountains with wildflowers decorating the landscape, or driving on Texas roads covered in bluebonnets, Indian paintbrush, and coreopsis in the spring. The combination of bluebonnets (Texas state flower) and Indian paintbrush (Wyoming state flower) I view as a sign my husband and I were meant to be together—or Wyoming and Texas are supposed to be together. There is something so wild and free about the two states yet also a feeling of being rooted in making homes with gardens, raising families, and nurturing communities, agriculture, and wild histories.

Grasses are a must for the artist gardener. Many of the ornamental varieties do very well here, producing a colorful bloom in the fall, which is perfect timing for decorating or fresh-cut fall arrangements. The grass stems are used in basketmaking, which is something I will do before I die. I love the sound grass makes when the wind whips through. I love the golden color in fall as the grass grows to maturity, gently and softly arching, softening its rigid lines. I love the smell of its sweetness and the waves it makes in a giant field as the wind blows through.

Native perennials and plants are essential, but living in the country, I have to use caution when planting them. Some native plants will take over like weeds, but I do include some varieties such as Turks Cap (every part of it is edible), American Beauty Berry (the birds' favorite food), Coreopsis, Salvia, Rudbeckia, and Guara, to name just a few. The big deal with native plants is that they keep the native population of insects, birds, and other wildlife healthy and prosperous.

The easiest and most ornamental perennials to plant are tropical. One in particular is Hamelia patens (firebush or hummingbird bush). I've seen it growing out of a crack in a rock! It grows huge—7 feet tall and wide every year—and dies completely back in the winter, even in our mildest winters. Hummingbirds swarm it in the fall. My friend Evelyn from Guatemala uses it in tea to help with symptoms of menstruation. She also taught me about the benefits of Tecoma stans (Esperanza or Yellow Bells). In her native land, they used Esperanza leaves in tea to naturally lower blood sugar.

The very first perennial I bought when I moved to Texas was Golden Dew Drops Duranta (Duranta erecta) because of the way it moved my soul. I had never seen a plant like it. It looked like a gentle weeping shrub covered in light blue-purple flowers that turned into golden yellow fruit in the fall. Decorating with the berries and clippings from our Christmas tree is gorgeous and brings me great joy.

Salvias are essential in Texas gardens. Salvia greggii will reseed itself gently and spread all over the garden. Black and Blue salvia is majestic with giant deep blue flowers. Mystic

Spires salvia is a dependable performer with tons of color and will not spread. Indigo spires come back year after year, blooming almost year-round.

Perennials produce flowers, just not as prolifically as annuals. But they are a necessary component in my fresh-cut arrangements. It's important to me to have clippings of flowers (annuals and perennials) with herbs and grasses in little vases around the house. In the winter I do clippings of branches, including holly with the berries in my arrangements. I could stare at them indefinitely, at the dinner table or by my bed. The arrangements do something to my heartbeat, slowing it down and calming my mind. Beautiful flowers, shrubs, herbs, and grasses I grow or find growing nearby bring me close to nature at all times.

Perennials are so easy to care for. Cutting them back twice a year is really all that is needed. This is usually the time I make my compost tea, which is what I fertilize with. However, I am human and get carried away with life, so adding any organic fertilizer is a good alternative. If harvesting medicinal roots such as valerian root, echinacea root, or ginger, it's best to do it in the fall on year two of the plant. Plants begin to put all their energy into the growth of their roots by November through February, which is why this is the time we see the most benefit from roots. The ideal time to plant perennials is in the fall when the soil is still warm from the summer but the air is cooling down. Perennials are like shrubs and trees in the way they focus most of their energy on their roots before they can begin growing above ground.

I suppose that is the same as humans. Before we can show external growth, we need to grow within, healing anything that afflicts us within so we can be strong, courageous, caring, and considerate.

Healing—that is the ultimate purpose of gardening. It is watching through observation how life works in unity with other living things. It requires patience. To harvest one root from echinacea, you must nurture it for two years. And when the two years arrive, it doesn't feel like it took very long at all. For me, I didn't really begin to grow until I had a family I needed to grow for. Probably like most people, I didn't have much invested in my own self-worth. I didn't live my life for the better. I just knew I didn't want to be bad. What I did wasn't considered taking care of myself; it was considered not dying. Now, when I give energy and care to plants, animals, and people, I receive energy and care back from all of them. I feel it in my mind, body, and spirit.

The Vegetable Garden

Large living things such as trees, shrubs, humans, animals, and garden soils all need three years to become healthy and resilient. Trees and shrubs focus all their energy for growth on their roots for the first full year. In year two, the energy is mostly focused on the roots and somewhat focused on external growth. By the third year, much less energy is spent on the roots, and the majority of energy is spent on external growth.

Humans are built the same way. The first year of their life is learning to fight off infections and building a healthy gut flora. That is why breastfeeding is so important, especially right before the milk comes in. Our bodies produce a yellow milk called colostrum that is very rich in nutrients, contains antibodies, and helps build the baby's digestive system by building cells and coating the intestines. That first full year of the baby's life is focused on building the immune system, brain, respiratory system, and digestive system. In the second year, we begin to see more outward growth with walking, talking, exploring, getting into trouble, and potty training. By the third year and on, growth continues on the inside but is much more noticeable on the outside with changes in physical features.

Soil is the same. The first year, whether it's an in-ground garden or raised bed, any soil added is new and needs to be nurtured. For the in-ground garden, adding compost helps with drainage and builds health of the soil. This is the first step. I encourage adding sand to raise the height of the soil, which keeps roots above sitting water. Compost builds the health and structure of the soil. Finding good compost is difficult, especially when you need bulk amounts. However, there are companies that source vegetables from local restaurants and tree and shrub clippings to build healthy compost for sale, which is an excellent alternative if you don't already have your own compost. Compost is like the colostrum from mother's milk. As long as no fungicide, herbicide, or pesticide is added, the beneficial fungi and bacteria will continue to grow and fight off viruses and fungi, and keep insects at bay. The first year the crop will be small, but there will be a crop. By year two, the crop will be much better, even making enough to store. By year three, the in-ground garden will make enough for the family with plenty to blanch, freeze, or can, with extra to share.

Planting a vegetable garden only became important to me when I began my family. Hearing stories about Roundup Ready plants being planted for grain crops, the seemingly huge spike in cancer, autism, birth defects, and ADHD scared me into becoming as organic as possible. Unfortunately, there were articles about even "organic" grains still having traces of toxic chemicals. I knew with a mother's heart that I had to protect my children by growing their food for them. And that's what I did. The garden became even more. I found if I showed my kids what flowers, berries, or sugar snaps were edible, they would go out grazing as a way to occupy much of their time and, in turn, interact with insects and reptilians. Essentially, they could watch life grow and unfold in front of their very eyes.

Now my girls harvest and munch on the bounty as a snack. It brings serenity to my soul to see them fully engaged, calm, absorbing nutrients and vitamin D from the sun, getting dirt under their fingernails, walking barefoot, and building their immune systems. The calm I see them experience is the most beautiful part of it all. I, too, enjoy walking barefoot through the gardens. My mind slows down almost like I drank a glass or two of wine. When I add five deep breaths, my mind focuses, and once again I am able to be productive.

I started off with a 5'x10' raised bed garden and planted other vegetables in my garden beds surrounding my house. After year three, the flower beds and one raised bed produced enough for our family, but I wanted more. I wanted to be able to fill our freezer with vegetables and not need to buy any at the store for the whole year. When we moved to the country with 2.5 acres, I felt I had a chance to make enough vegetables to meet my freezer goal. My husband built me four 4'x6'x2' raised beds using treated lumber, and six years later they are still in good condition. I like the low maintenance of raised beds. It's easier to manage the weeds. Weeds bring in insects, which bring in disease.

We built the beds in a 20'x20' area that we covered with 4 inches of compacted crushed granite. My husband built a 4-foot-tall fence with hog wire and posts around that to keep rabbits, armadillos, and other unwanted animals out. It was beautiful and still is, but it is also a work in progress. Our biggest hurdle was the weeds that loved growing in the crushed granite. I am against the use of weed killer, especially where we grow our food. Pulling the weeds was a six-day-a-week job and way too much work. Remembering that weeds love high bacterial soil and hate high fungal soil, I switched my practices and added 4 inches of hardwood mulch. This had to work. And it did, but mulch breaks down, creating great soil for weeds to grow. So I added a thick layer of pine straw, which has greatly helped suppress the weeds. These don't break down as easily, and pine needles are allelopathic (producing a chemical prohibiting the growth of other plants). That is the how pine trees survive. They are not good at competition with other plants, so when they drop their needles, a chemical from the needles is released that prevents other plants from growing. The smell from the pine needles instantly transports me to the mountains. Oh, how I love nature!

Again, the four beds weren't enough. I was able to blanch and freeze some vegetables, and we had enough to eat fresh for six months out of the year. But my real goal, I soon realized, could only be met with an in-ground garden.

Items Needed for a Manageable and Easy In-Ground Garden

- A small tractor with a tiller and row pulling attachment
- Weaved plastic weed barrier. This may seem totally unnatural and not like something I would suggest, but the biggest issue in our climate is weeds, and weeds bring insects that bring disease. Weeds have been the only reason I gave up on my gardens.
- Drip water system and sprinkler system
- Access to homemade compost
- Power Planter Auger 3"x36"

I love vegetable gardening. At first it was to provide proper nutrition for my family, and then it became the peace I needed in my life. It worked as therapy for my mind and soul. It taught me how to be thankful and give myself grace when a crop didn't do as well as I hoped. I receive so much joy seeing the new buds and vegetables begin to develop. Vegetable gardening gives me a sense of independence. By our hands and hard work, we could survive anything. Gardening is a form of meditation and physical activity. It is during gardening that I have my long conversations with God, mostly thanking him for this wonderful life. Sometimes I listen to a book on tape, transporting my mind somewhere else, or I jam out to music and sing my favorite songs.

As I water, gently touching each plant, my eyes observe and my mind makes sense of what my eyes see. My ears are in tune to any sounds, especially in the morning or evening. The morning brings abundant life to the garden. Bees are hard at work going in and out of each flower, covering themselves in pollen. I have seen a bee so full of pollen that it could barely fly, taking a break on a leaf with fresh dew drops to have a drink. In the evening, insects are busy eating the leaves. This is the best time to search for caterpillars. You can hear hornworms chewing the leaves of tomatoes. That is also the time to agitate leaf-footed stink bugs with water and shake them off the plants into soapy water (Dawn dish soap works the best).

We live in a world where we no longer need to wait for anything. Groceries, food, and goods made in China can be delivered to our door in no time at all by pressing a button. But the vegetable garden takes patience. You have to wait, but all the life experienced in that wait provides instant gratification.

Gardening is a uniquely personal labor of love. There are always new opportunities to learn and many different ways to approach and combat challenges. There is no one right way and no perfect way to garden. I've learned not to believe people who have the answer to everything. The more I learn, the more questions I have, and the only way to get them answered is by implementing what I think may work.

January	February
Black Beans (seed)	Asparagus (plants)
Beets (seed)	Beets (seed)
Bok Choy (seed/plant)	Black Beans (seed)
Broccoli (plant)	Bok Choy (plant)
Cabbage (plant)	Collards (plant)
Carrot (seed)	Kale (plant)
Chinese Cabbage (seed)	Kohlrabi (plant)
Chinese Snow Peas (seed)	Lettuce (seed/plant)
Collards (plant)	Multiplying Onion (bulbs)
Kale (plant)	Mustard Greens (seed)
Lettuce (seed/plant)	Spinach (plant)
Leek (bulbs)	Strawberries (plant)
Multiplying Onion (bulbs)	Tomato (seed/plant)
Mustard Greens (seed)	Turnips (seed)
Potato (seed)	
Radish (seed)	
Spinach (seed/plant)	
Strawberries (plant)	
Sugar Snap Peas (seed)	
Turnips (seed)	

March	April
Acorn Squash (seed/plant)	Cantaloupe (plant)
Butternut Squash (seed/plant)	Corn (seed)
Cantaloupe (seed/plant)	Cucumber (plant)
Corn (seed)	Eggplant (plant)
Cucumber (seed)	Green Beans Bush (seed)
Eggplant (plant)	Okra (seed/plant)
Green Beans Bush (seed)	Pepper (plant)
Lettuce (seed/plant)	Peanut (seed)
Mustard Greens (seed)	Tomatillo (plant)
Pepper (seed/plant)	Watermelon (seed)
Tomatillo (seed/plant)	Yellow Squash (seed/plant)
Tomato (plant)	Zucchini (seed/plant)
Yellow Squash (seed/plant)	
Zucchini (seed/plant)	

May	June
Cream Peas (seed)	Cream Peas (seed)
Cucumber (plant)	Purple Hull Peas (seed)
Eggplant (plant)	Sweet Potato (plant)
Gourds, edible (seed)	Zipper Peas (seed)
Okra (seed/plant)	
Peanut (seed)	
Pepper (plant)	
Purple Hull Peas (seed)	
Sweet Potato (plant)	
Zipper Peas (seed)	

July	August
Cream Peas (seed)	Black Bean Bush (seed)
Okra (plant)	Green Bean Bush (seed)
Purple Hull Peas (seed)	Japanese Cucumber (seed)
	Sweet Potato (plant)
	Tomato (plant)
	Yellow Squash (seed)
	Zucchini (seed)

September	October
Turnips (seed)	Artichoke (plant)
	Bok Choy (seed/plant)
	Broccoli (seed/plant)
	Brussels Sprouts (plant)
	Cabbage (seed/plant)
	Carrots (seed)
	Cauliflower (seed/plant)
	Collards (seed/plant)
	Kale (seed/plant)
	Lettuce (seed/plant)
	Mustard Greens (seed/plant)
	Spinach (seed/plant)
	Swiss Chard (seed/plant)
	Turnips (seed)

November	December
Bok Choy (plant)	Beet (seed)
Broccoli (plant)	Cabbage (plant)
Brussels Sprouts (plant)	Carrots (seed)
Cabbage (seed/plant)	Collards (plant)
Carrots (seed)	Kale (seed/plant)
Cauliflower (plant)	Lettuce (seed/plant)
Collards (plant)	Multiplying Onion (bulbs)
Garlic (clove)	Mustard Greens (seed/plant)
Kale (seed/plant)	Onion (bulbs)
Lettuce (seed/plant)	Potato (seed)
Mustard Greens (seed/plant)	Snow Pea (seed)
Onion (bulbs)	Spinach (seed/plant)
Snow Peas (seed)	Strawberries (plant)
Spinach (seed/plant)	Sugar Snap Pea (seed)
Strawberries (bareroot/plant)	Swiss Chard (seed/plant)
Swiss Chard (seed/plant)	Turnips (seed)
Turnips (seed)	

Gardening by the Moon Phase

The moon is an incredible force that has an impact on fertilization, migration, tides, blooming, and soil moisture levels. I long to be more like the creatures living outside with their circadian rhythm in perfect harmony with nature and natural forces. Part of me feels like I am in rhythm with the moon. Worms, along with fish and some crabs, can sense the phases of the moon using this instinct to trigger a species-wide reproduction. Both the full moon and the new moon affect the rising tide levels, including the size of waves. From the moment of a new moon when no moon is present in the night sky to a full moon, the moisture levels slowly rise as the moon pulls moisture from deep within the soil toward the surface. Different crops should be planted at different moon phases.

- *New Moon (no moon in the sky, but the gravitational pull of moisture toward the surface is strong):* Plant herbs, flowers, leafy vegetables (spinach, mustard or collard greens, lettuce), cabbage, broccoli, and cauliflower.

- *Waxing Moon (as the moon begins to get bigger starting as a sliver—I like to call this "God's thumbnail"—about 5–7 days before it's full):* Plant fruits, beans, peas, tomatoes, peppers, eggplants, watermelon, cantaloupe, squash, zucchini, cucumbers, loofa, and corn.
- *Full Moon-Waning Moon (directly after full moon until new moon when the moon is pulling moisture from the surface down to the deep parts of the soil):* Plant bulbs (including flowering bulbs), potatoes, carrots, turnips, radishes, beets, and onions. It's also a great time to harvest, fertilize, pull weeds, and prune.

The *Farmers' Almanac* follows this process, and so have I for the most part. There are times I will stray from the moon cycle, and I still have success. However, it helps to organize planting, which helps me be a more productive gardener. I don't consider myself very structured or a by-the-book rule-follower, so it's good for me to add some organization to my life. There's that balance thing again. We can't have yin without the yang, good without the bad, made by nature and made by man, organic and synthetic, Eastern medicine and Western medicine. Such is true with gardening. It's nice to have guidelines but with flexibility in order to be creative.

❧ ☙

Weed Control in Gardens

The only thing that makes me stop gardening is weeds. They are good and bad at the same time, and just when you think you have everything under control, it rains, and weeds take over overnight. They are good because our bees and other pollinators are attracted to the weeds' flowers. They can also act as a groundcover to protect our soil from intense sun rays and erosion. They are bad because they grow viciously tall and wide with deep, wide roots that compete for the water. They bring in all insects, good and bad, which then bring in viruses and diseases. Our garden is large, 60'x40'. It is my goal to use my resources wisely and cost effectively to suppress the weeds.

Please keep in mind again that I don't know everything. I am still trying to figure out what works best for me, my crop schedule, and the amount of effort I have available for my gardening projects. Also, Mother Nature dictates when to plant. If I want to plant potatoes during a torrential rainy season, that's probably not a good idea. I plant my seeds if it has been sunny and warm for a full week after winter weather, giving the soil time to heat up, and the next week is supposed to be rainy. What I have learned I have also practiced. Some of it has been accidental, some are secrets shared with me by others, and some are purely instinctual. I have succeeded and failed. The one thing that has proved consistent is that I do not actually have any of the control. I can think I do, but the one thing I can count on is that some years certain crops do better than others, and the next year may not be the same. That's why versatility in crops will guarantee my time, money, and energy have not been wasted.

The following methods of gardening are my observations from different techniques I've implemented so far to maintain the most organic, highest-production, and healthiest plants.

- *Cover Crops:* They maintain soil structure when the main crops are not being grown. Because of our climate, there is only one time of year this is absolutely necessary: during the summer. I use legumes such as peas or beans as a cover crop because of their nitrogen-fixing abilities, which means those crops are capable of taking nitrogen from the air through its foliage and sending it down to its roots where special bacteria attracted to the roots will implant themselves, turning the nitrogen into a form (ammonia or ammonia nitrate) that other plants will use as fertilizer. For the summer months, purple hull peas are the easiest legumes to grow. They love our heat and humidity when most other crops disintegrate. Mustard greens are another excellent cover crop for cool seasons (anywhere between September through June).

- *Crop Rotation:* This is refraining from planting the same crop in the same row season after season. This practice helps prevent disease and insect populations from getting out of control. For example, plant green beans followed by melons followed by spinach and cauliflower followed by yellow squash and zucchini followed by purple hull peas followed by strawberries and onions and tomatoes and radishes followed by cream peas followed by broccoli followed by mustard greens followed by potatoes followed by purple hull peas followed by black beans and lettuce followed by green beans—and then begin the cycle all over again.
- *Low Till System:* Till the soil little to none. Tilling exposes the abiotic and biotic material to the sun and aridity, which lowers the population of the microorganisms with each till. We till once a year when it's a cloudy day after the summer harvest, usually in August or September. Tilling also helps bury weed seeds way below the soil where they don't get enough of their needs met and eventually

die. It also helps put nitrogen in the soil from the foliage of plants and grasses that have been tilled into the soil. Finally, tilling breaks up the soil and loosens compaction, creating a healthy environment for roots to grow.

- *Mulch:* Mulch helps maintain a consistent soil temperature and moisture level. I need 3 yards of a good non-dyed mulch for my garden, which is around $100. I've used hay, but the hay quickly became moldy. Pine straw is the best option, but to cover my garden would have a $300 price tag. Compost works as mulch but breaks down quickly and needs to be reapplied at least four times a year. I make an excellent compost twice a year and use it for all our gardens. What has proved to work best for me is weaved plastic weed barrier for the first few years to discourage weeds from growing. Once I've pulled the rows and laid out the plastic weed barrier, I burn holes in it where I want the plants to live. I like that it does an excellent job at weed suppression, and the extra heat that it traps speeds up crop time. I've had full harvests before Christmas, which was lucky when a surprise freeze came through on Christmas Eve one year and wiped everyone's crops out except mine. I still use compost to cover each of the rows and then cover the rows with the weaved plastic. The plastic lasts in our Texas sun for years, making it economical and efficient. Every summer I do worry and stress if the soil is too hot under the black weaved barrier, but after testing my soil under the microscope, everything seems to be healthy and in complete working condition. It's only my mind telling me it's not working.

Prepping the Garden

Soil is the lifeblood of plants. Without healthy soil, the immune systems of plants are weak and susceptible to pathogens, stress, and insects. When plants are under stress, they release a pheromone that attracts insects to come and attack.

Our soil is rich and compacted. When it's hot and dry, giant deep cracks form as the cells of the soil shrink and tighten as they gear into survival mode. I like to believe the cracks are earth's way of opening up its heart to allow rain to fall deep into its aquifers. Adding sand helps build the soil up higher to avoid drowning and assists with drainage. However, if you add only one thing, let that one thing be compost. Compost adds microbes into the soil to build its health, breaks up compaction, assists with resilience to pathogens, regulates the soil temperatures from either getting too hot or too cold, reduces water loss, breaks up heavy metals, and feeds the roots of plants. Add compost in every hole and as mulch with every planting. The final addition for a new garden is a 1/4-inch layer of earthworm castings. It's nature's fertilizer, enhancing seed germination, flowering, and fruit production. It also curbs certain plant diseases and inhibits pests. Till in the sand, spread fertilizer, pull rows, cover rows with compost, and then cover the entire garden with weaved plastic, burning holes where desired planting will happen. Set up drip irrigation and sprinklers.

Building a simple fence around the garden helps keep out squirrels, rabbits, armadillos, deer, dogs, raccoons, and cats. The 4-foot-tall fence around our raised bed garden is much more intricate than the 4-foot fence around our in-ground garden. For the raised bed garden, we used 4"x4" and 2"x4" treated lumber with 12.5-gauge hog wire. It is very sweet, and I get compliments on it all the time. The in-ground garden fence is much simpler with T-posts and 12.5-gauge hog wire with a foot of chicken wire at the base to keep rodents out of the garden. I imagine if I lived where there were deer, I would build my fences taller at a height of at least 6 feet. And now it's time to plant!

The Veggie List

Here is your list of veggies with some of easy recipes and secrets I've learned to make you a successful gardener.

- *Artichoke:* Surprisingly, this is the very best trap crop I have ever planted. When tomatoes are beginning to ripen, they are highly susceptible to the leaf-footed stink bug that will destroy an entire crop in a matter of days. Artichokes are much more appetizing to them, and they will attack it instead of the more vulnerable crops. Artichoke is a gorgeous fall, winter, and spring plant. It will die back to the ground in the heat of the summer to reemerge again in the fall. The foliage is a gentle silver-green, and the size of the plant is stunning. It looks gorgeous mixed with snapdragons, dianthus, marigolds, and tulips. The fruit is edible and loaded with fiber.
- *Arugula:* This is the first year I planted seeds around the perimeter of my in-ground garden with the hopes of pushing weeds out. It worked like a

charm, and I reaped a bountiful harvest of fresh arugula to mix with my salads or eat fresh. I love its spicy flavor that bites at my tongue when eaten fresh picked in the garden. It's the first thing I do when visiting my garden. I look at the arugula with its dainty white flowers that are attracting all the bees and other beneficial insects to my garden, and then I eat a few leaves to stimulate my senses. It is extremely hardy to the cold and reseeds itself easily.

- *Beets:* These are preferably grown in a raised bed garden, but I've grown them in both gardens. They are incredibly high in nutrients and have a distinct earthy flavor. They can be fermented, which is awesome. Fermentation creates all those probiotics our bodies need, but the way I love to eat them is roasted with olive oil, salt, and pepper, served warm in salad with homemade rosemary balsamic vinaigrette.

Warm Beet Salad

- Dark green lettuce mixture (spinach, arugula, chickweed and lettuce)
- Goat cheese
- Pecans
- Chopped red onion
- Chopped cucumbers
- Warm beets

Preheat oven to 400 degrees.

Scrub beet roots, peel, and cut into bite-sized pieces. Mix in a bowl with 2 tablespoons olive oil, salt, and pepper.

Bake, covered, for 30 minutes.

Place lettuce in a bowl, and add pecans, cucumbers, and onion. Mix in some Rosemary Vinaigrette and top with roasted beets and crumbled goat cheese.

Rosemary Vinaigrette

- 3 fresh sprigs of rosemary
- 2 teaspoons fresh oregano
- 2 teaspoons fresh mint
- 2 teaspoons fresh chives
- 1 teaspoon fresh winter savory
- 2 garlic cloves, chopped
- 1/2 cup first cold-pressed olive oil
- 1/3 cup aged balsamic vinegar
- 2 tablespoons water
- 1 tablespoon local honey
- Salt and pepper to taste

Mix all ingredients together using a whisk, or if you're lazy like me, put it all in a jar and shake, shake, shake. Let it marinate for at least 4 hours before using.

- *Black Beans:* Once I learned I could grow black beans here, nothing stopped me. Like all legumes, black beans mend the soil while providing the most delicious crop ever with loads of fiber. Black beans are ready for harvest when the shells lighten in color and have a gentle purple vein. The beans inside will be light purple to dark purple. I've dried them out before but still managed to get some mold while in storage, although it was easily washed off. Instead of storing dried beans, I like to blanch fresh beans, dry them, and then freeze them.

Easy Black Beans

- 2 cups black beans, rinsed
- 1/2 cup butter
- 2 teaspoons salt

Place all ingredients in a stainless-steel pot. Cover the beans with enough water until the level is 1/2 inch above the beans.

Bring to a boil and then reduce the heat to a simmer for 2-1/2 hours, until the beans are tender and water is no longer excessive. Stir occasionally.

Remove from heat. Serve as a side dish or wrap in tortillas with fresh grated cheese.

- *Blackberries:* Triple Crown is the absolute best I have ever grown. All you need is one plant. Every year it will come back more and more. It's thornless and produces from spring until the first frost. It makes enough to share with the birds (which keeps them away from other crops) and the chickens. The giant fruit is a tart yet sweet tasting. They are ready for harvesting when the berries easily fall off the stem when gently moved back and forth. We eat them fresh and in pies, and I make a seedless jam with them that I use instead of syrup on pancakes. Storing frozen berries for future snacks.

Seedless Blackberry Jam

- 2 or more pounds of rinsed blackberries
- 2 tablespoons butter
- 1/4 cup freshly squeezed lemon juice
- 1 cup sugar (I've made it with honey as well)

Combine all ingredients in a stainless-steel pot over medium-low heat.

Cook down until ingredients have decreased in size by half.

Using a handheld mixer, mash up the blackberry mixture.

Strain the mashed blackberries in a metal sieve into sterilized jam jars while still hot. Make sure all jam has been wiped clean from the lip of the jar, and place a new jar lid on the hot jar. Close tightly with the band, flip upside down for 10 minutes, and then return it to right side up. You will know the jar is sealed when an indentation forms on the lid.

- *Broccoli:* This is one of the easiest crops to grow and such a wonderful giver. After harvesting the main head, do not pull the plant out. No matter which variety you plant, they all make smaller florets that provide many more meals and make an excellent addition to stir fries. It seems each plant will produce large heads all at the same time, but blanching, drying, and freezing them make this an excellent veggie to eat year-round. Do not plant broccoli with cauliflower as they will compete for nutrients, and cauliflower enjoys more water than broccoli. Sometimes I'll let a few broccoli plants go to flower; the bees really enjoy them.
- *Cabbage:* I often plant a whole row of cabbage. I love experimenting with fermentation and making sauerkraut. The best time to harvest is right after a cold snap when the flavor is the sweetest. Along with broccoli and cauliflower, cabbage does not need to be covered in freezing weather. It lasts a long time in the refrigerator and on the plant itself.

Coleslaw

- 1/2 head of cabbage, thinly sliced
- 1 red onion, thinly sliced
- 3–5 carrots, peeled and shredded
- 1/2 cup mayonnaise
- 1 tablespoon sugar
- 2 teaspoons Kosher salt (more if needed)
- 1 tablespoon celery seed
- 1/4 cup red wine vinegar
- Freshly ground pepper to taste

In a large bowl add mayonnaise, sugar, salt, celery seed, and vinegar. Mix well. Add cabbage, onion, and carrots, and mix. Add salt and pepper to taste. Let rest for at least one hour. It tastes even better the second day.

- *Cantaloupe:* Some years I have great success with cantaloupe and some years not so much. But when they do produce, they are totally worth the wait. The flavor is unlike any store-bought cantaloupe. They are so filled with juice it just drips down your chin onto your clothing. Chickens go crazy over the seeds.
- *Carrots:* Carrots are grown best in raised beds. They can even handle quite a bit of shade. Keep them moist after planting for about a week, and then water only when needed. When the orange

tops stick out of the ground, they are ready to harvest. One of the best smells in the world is a freshly picked carrot. The herbal-musky-earthy-man smell of soil mixed with the sweet carrot fragrance rushes to my brain, sending instant calm throughout my body. Wiping off the dirt and eating it fresh out of the ground is one of the best spring treats. It is at this point that the flavor of the carrot is at its highest point. It loses its intensity the longer it has been pulled from the earth. Storage of carrots is incredibly easy. Snap off the leaves, shake off as much dirt as possible, and cool them to room temperature before storing in an unsealed plastic bag in the refrigerator. They will last like this for several months. Nothing says spring like carrot cake with cream cheese frosting.

Carrot Cake

- 2 cups flour
- 2 cups sugar
- 1 teaspoon baking powder
- 1 teaspoon baking soda
- 1 teaspoon cinnamon
- 1/2 teaspoon salt
- 3 cups grated carrots
- 4 eggs room temperature
- 1 cup melted coconut oil

Preheat oven to 350 degrees.

Grease a 9”x13” pan and then flour it.

Mix all dry ingredients together in a large bowl.

Mix all wet ingredients together in a smaller bowl.

Add wet ingredients to dry ingredients. Stir until blended making sure not to over-mix. Pour into the pan and bake for 60 minutes. You will know when the cake is complete by poking a toothpick in the thickest part. If it comes out dry, the cake is done cooking.

Cream Cheese Frosting

- 1 8-ounce package of cream cheese at room temperature
- 1/4 cup butter, softened
- 1 teaspoon vanilla
- 2 cups powdered sugar, sifted

Combine cream cheese, butter, and vanilla in a mixing bowl. Mix until smooth.

Add powdered sugar 1/2 cup at a time.

Apply to a fully cooled cake.

- *Cauliflower:* It loves water and is an excellent companion plant for spinach. My mother-in-law taught me to clothespin the large leaves together over the flower when it either rains a lot or when we have a freeze to help keep the vegetable pure white. Blanching and freezing is recommended for long-term storage. My favorite way to prepare this delightful vegetable is steamed with Julia Child's lemon butter sauce.

- *Citrus:* Meyer lemons and satsuma are essential for every yard. They are both relatively cold-hardy and will thrive when planted on the south side of the house where the house can protect them from freezing northern winds in the winter. Like all things, it takes three years to establish the roots so they are strong enough to produce fruit. Pull all the fruit off the first year. All citrus are treated with a systemic insecticide that lasts one year and disperses everywhere, including the fruit. Citrus greening is a serious bacterial infection spread by an insect called the Asian citrus psyllid. It is highly contagious and is the reason there are such intense regulations on the sale and commercial growing of citrus. You may see one or two fruits the second year of growing citrus organically, but the third year you will begin to be able to share your crop. Growing citrus organically is the most effective way to prevent insects and diseases. Having a healthy immune system through using compost, fertilizing a couple times a year, and making sure there is adequate drainage and consistent watering helps prevent the plant from stressing.

During Hurricane Harvey, my Meyer lemon came in handy. As a transplant from Wyoming, I was not accustomed to hurricanes, but more than that, it was the hundreds of tornados that come with it. My husband was working as a lineman for CenterPoint Energy, and I was left to fend the storms alone with my two young children. My neighbor, and now really close friend, was in the same boat. She was a transplant from Illinois. Her husband is a fireman, and she was left to fend for herself and her very young girls. We banded together, made margaritas and popcorn, and watched tornados touch down all around us. But those margaritas were the best and still are to this day.

Hurricane Harvey Margaritas (made by the glass)

- 1-1/2 fresh green or yellow Meyer lemons (even the green ones contain excellent flavor with high amounts of juice). Meyer lemons are known for their vast amounts of juice and their sweet citrus flavor used as a delicacy in high-end restaurants.
- One shot of 100% pure blue agave tequila (I prefer the well-aged añejo or reposado)
- One shot of orange liqueur (Triple Sec or Gran Marnier)

Pour all ingredients, starting with the orange liqueur and ending with the lemons, over a full glass of ice. Stir and drink.

- *Cucumber (Pickling):* The skin on these are slightly bitter. Shaving off half the skin makes for a better flavor when eating them fresh. But the thick, bitter skin of the pickling variety is ideal for pickling or fermenting. My mother-in-law gave me a very old German crock to do just that: fermenting. My first time using it was on my winter cabbage crop. I completely messed it up and ended up throwing away the final product because I closed the lid and didn't check back until six weeks later. Then I did a little research and learned that it is necessary to continue to check the progress daily and remove any mold. I made a batch of fermented cucumbers with fresh homegrown dill seed head and peeled garlic, and it only took one week. It was amazing! Cucumber beetles are the primary pest but can easily be killed by applying diatomaceous earth spray to the affected plants. As the insects crawl over it, they will be gently cut open and dehydrate to death.

Fermented food has become a growing craze in the United States in the last five years or so. It is said that fermented foods build and strengthen gut flora, which helps with increased energy, increased immune system responses, decreased depression, and decreased inflammation. I believe that to be true, but I also believe that everything must be done in moderation. After the use of antibiotics, it is important to rebuild the good bacteria in your gut. But if you're already healthy with no issues, perhaps leave well enough alone. Don't fix it if it ain't broke.

Fermented Pickles

- 1 heavy crock. There is a reason old German crocks last forever with their incredibly thick walls and heavy lid. My husband bought me a crock with a water seal lid. I loved that one but only had the privilege of using it twice before it broke because of how thin it was. I was impressed by the ease and pure flavor of the fermented products coming from the water-sealed crock, so when my mother-in-law gifted me a new one for my birthday, I quickly put it to use.
- As many pickle-sized fresh cucumbers as possible, rinsed. Discard (or feed to the chickens) any that have gone bad by being a little soft.
- Fresh dill flower heads, with or without the seeds and foliage
- Several fresh grape leaves, rinsed

- Pints of distilled or reverse osmosis water (do not use filtered or city water as it contains bacteria-killing chemicals, and the whole point is to produce bacteria)
- Kosher salt
- Whole peeled garlic cloves (quantity is up to you; I use a lot)
- Whole cayenne peppers, rinsed

In the crock, lay a layer of cucumbers with fresh dill seed heads and garlic and a cayenne pepper.

Dissolve 2 tablespoons Kosher salt in a pint of water. Pour it in the crock so the cucumbers are fully submerged.

Continue this process until all cucumbers are in the crock.

Cover the cucumbers with a layer of grape leaves.

Place a plate over the leaves and press down, using a rock as a weight.

Cover the crock with a flour sack towel and then the lid.

Check daily and remove any mold (gold, white, green, even black); however, if it smells bad, something went wrong. I'm not sure what went wrong because this is a very simple process, and if you check it daily, you will be just fine.

After six or seven days, be brave and taste test a pickle. If it tastes like a pickle, it is time to jar them up in sterilized jars and store them in the refrigerator for several months—or pressure seal the jars, which can then be stored in the pantry for a very long time.

If using a water-sealed crock, use the same method minus the towel, plate and rock. Just use weights on top of the grape leaves. Leave it untouched in a cool dark space for about four weeks, refilling the water around the lid daily. Do not run out of water. You will know when they are ready when the water on the seal stops bubbling.

- *Cucumber, Japanese:* These are best planted in the fall. The end of August is the ideal time to plant the seeds. The long and tender fruit has such a delicate sweet taste that it's not necessary to peal any of the outer skin. This is by far my most delicious variety of fresh cucumber for eating.
- *Eggplant (ichiban or Other Long Slender Asian Varieties):* I had never been a fan of eggplant. Growing up and all the way until my thirties, every time I ate eggplant, my tongue tingled and I swore I was allergic to it. But when I had my first garden here in Texas, I grew one plant and was very impressed with its production. I had plenty of slender, tender, mild-flavored fruit ready to harvest at just the right time (the same time I was

harvesting my fresh tomato and zucchini crops). My husband had bou*ght Julia Child's Mastering the Art of French Cooking* cookbook after watching the *Julie & Julia* movie. I knew her recipe for ratatouille involved those three ingredients, so I proceeded to try my hand at some real French cooking. It was quite the process but so incredibly worth the work. The ingredients for the dish are eggplant, zucchini, tomato, olive oil, and Kosher salt. That's it! I had never tasted such a wonderful stew, and it was all organically grown from my garden. To this day I'm not sure if it's the love I include in growing, harvesting, and cooking, but I'll be damned if my food isn't the best-tasting in the world. Last night I made roasted eggplant with homegrown onion, homegrown tomato, and homegrown basil, roasted in avocado oil and Kosher salt. When completed, I reduced some balsamic vinegar and drizzled it with olive oil over the dish. *Delicious!*

- *Garlic (Soft Neck):* I've only grown this one time and keep meaning to grow it again. I had just an okay production in my raised bed, but I think the production would be greater if grown in the ground or in a container where water can be managed. They like to be on the drier side. Plant them in November after soaking the pealed cloves. Plant them in the area of the garden that doesn't receive too much water. They are ready for harvest (usually around June) when the foliage has bent over in a 90-degree angle. Braid the harvested cloves together and air-dry them indoors with good ventilation. Many people use garlic to cure issues. For example, slicing a clove in half and rubbing it on the sinuses is supposed to relieve sinus pressure. Fun fact: Eating garlic cloves before bed gives you lucid dreams.

- *Grapes:* There has only been one year that I have had a great harvest of grapes, but I know there will be more in store as the vines age. Champanel is the variety I planted. The skin is thick and sour, there are seeds, and the flesh of the fruit is sweet and almost gummy-like—nature's sweet and sour candy. It's recommended to plant roses at the end of the row of vines. Roses are the best companion plants for grapes because the roses show signs of diseases before they have a chance to spread to the precious fruit. Also, aphids and other insects are more attracted to the roses, helping prevent attacks on the sensitive vines. Grapes are susceptible to the grape leaf roller caterpillar that has attacked my grapes every year. I usually let the leaf rollers do their business even if they eat all the foliage. Only one time did I produce enough fruit to do anything of substance with it, and grape jam was the result. Wow! I have never made a better flavored jam. It was so good. I was selfish and only shared it with my husband and kids. I was a novice when I planted grapes. I've had to relocate them because they grow so large. Where I have them now is not ideal, and I will need to relocate them again. They need a designated space that gets plenty of airflow for them to grow large, wild, and free. As they are susceptible to diseases, planting on the north side of anything is not good. Plant the vines in a tilled-ground garden enriched with compost and expanded shale. A strong trellis is required—and roses!

Grape Jam Pectin-Free (Works for All Jams)

- 2 pounds grapes, rinsed and skin cut with an X on one end
- 1 cup sugar or honey, whichever you prefer
- 1/3 cup freshly squeezed lemons
- 6 canning jars, sanitized with new lids
- Wide-mouth funnel, ladle, and stainless-steel strainer
- Cooling rack

In a stainless-steel or copper pot add grapes, sugar or honey, and freshly squeezed lemon juice. Cook down until saucy looking.

Strain liquid, removing all the seeds and skin, and return to heat until boiling.

While the mixture is hot, use a wide-mouth funnel and a ladle to fill sanitized jars. Make sure no juice gets on the rim of the jars. Place a new lid on the top of the jar and tighten the ring. Flip the jars upside down on a cooling rack for 5 minutes and then flip upright.

You will know you have created a seal when the button on the center of the lid has recessed.

- *Lettuce:* When harvesting lettuce, only cut off either the top half or just the leaves you want to use. Lettuce will continue to grow and produce more if it's harvested this way. Storing lettuce is easy. Rinse the harvest, shake off as much water as possible, or use a lettuce spinner, and store in an open plastic bag or sealed container. It will store in the refrigerator like this for several weeks. However, the longer it's stored, the less nutrition it will provide. When lettuce begins to bolt (one thick stalk grows in the very center with a few sporadic leaves), it is no longer tender and tasty. But I let them bolt, flower, and then go to seed to see what pops up the following season.
- *Mustard Greens (Florida Broadleaf Preferred, but Any Variety Will Do):* This is by far one of the most

essential crops to grow. First, the nutrient content is incredibly dense. Second, the chemical released in the soil by its roots, called glucosinolates, will kill nematodes (the bad kind that attack potato crops). It's perfect for a cover crop before planting potatoes. It's a good idea to plant these in a row where the intention is to plant your potato crop or any other root crops affected by nematodes. One of my favorite things to do while walking in the garden is to chew a piece of fresh mustard greens. Its intense horseradish bite stimulates all my senses and makes me tear up just a little. It's also one of my favorite party tricks to have people try a fresh piece. It brings so much joy to watch kids and adults struggle with the bite. For our family, a classic mustard green dish done the Southern way is unbeatable. We all devour it. In fact, it was one of the first vegetable dishes my youngest would not just eat but would overconsume.

Southern Mustard Greens

- 1 very large bunch of fresh, rinsed, dried, deveined mustard greens, chopped
- 1 whole onion, diced
- 2 slices of bacon, thinly sliced
- 2 cups homemade bone broth
- Salt and pepper to taste

On medium-high heat, fry bacon in a Dutch oven until golden brown.

Add onion and cook until softened, stirring continuously.

Add mustard greens, one handful at a time, cooking down after each handful while stirring until all have been added.

Add bone broth and cook until boiling. Cover and reduce heat to low, occasionally stirring. Keep this up for 3–4 hours.

Salt and pepper to taste, and enjoy!

- *Onion:* At first my husband complained that I added too much onion to everything. I grew a lot of onion every year in my garden, and he tried to always give it away to people. But now, that is no longer the case. I don't know when the shift took place, but he enjoys onion now. And thank God! Onion is amazing for men's sexual health. Onions are ready to be harvested when the green stems have bent over in a 90-degree angle. Red onions are the best producers and are so good for your overall health by lowering blood sugar and protecting against some strains of cancer.
- *Peppers:* Growing peppers in raised beds or containers where they receive partial shade is ideal,

at least for me and the types of peppers I prefer such as sweet peppers. I haven't been extremely successful with most bell peppers, but I do grow banana peppers and eat them like bell peppers and gypsy peppers, a small bell pepper. I also grow cayenne peppers for some heat. The older the plant, the spicier the pepper. I have had some peppers for two years. That's another benefit to growing in a pot, for protection from freezes.

- *Potatoes:* There is certainly a trick to growing these. La Soda red potatoes have been a high yield variety with very few issues. However, they are not bullet-proof and still have a vulnerability to nematodes (which can be prevented by planting mustard greens in the same row for an early fall production and amending the bed with ample diatomaceous earth before planting) and potato blight. It's just because of the area we live in, with high humidity, warm days and cool nights. Blight can be slowed by cutting the infected leaves off and throwing them in the trash or burn pit (no composting). Once the soil in the garden is healthy and fully alive with microbes viruses are less prevalent. My mother-in-law shared with me her father's secret to potato growing. After cutting the seed potatoes in half with at least two eyes per half, lay them out indoors for one to two weeks to let them scab over or cure. When planting, dip each potato in wood ash, which can't have any other type of product in it. I use my husband's barbecue ashes for this. Wood ash is a natural fungicide and helps prevent the bulb from rotting. Another essential step for a bumper crop is to raise the soil up over the plant when it is 12 inches tall. We have a row puller attachment for our tractor that makes this step super easy for us, but if that isn't available, using a hoe does the job perfectly. I like to think of this step as aerating the soil, loosening it, and tickling the plant, thus encouraging it to be more productive. Potatoes are ready to harvest after they have bloomed and when digging in the soil a little you see that they are ready. The potato used as the seed is the ultimate mother of all vegetables. It gives its entire life and energy to make the babies and will die once it has given everything.

Potatoes as Treatment for Warts

I believe in signs. I believe God puts signs in our path when we need them. My twenty-one-year subscription to the world's most interesting magazine has proven fruitful many times. My daughter, a young school-aged girl, had a wart on her hand. I remember when I was a girl I had a couple warts on my hands as well. My mom treated them with a liquid that froze them off. One day as I was reading an article in my magazine, I saw that someone had written about a cure for warts she had learned about from her Mennonite background. On a full moon, cut a potato in half and place one half on the wart for about a minute. Take that half outside and place it under a water spout on the south side of the house. The first time I tried this suggestion I did it on the day after the full moon. Nothing happened to the wart. The second time I tried it, I made sure it was during a full moon. Within a week, the wart was gone. Of course, I was skeptical and thought it could have just been a coincidence. But wouldn't you know, a few months later, my daughter had a plantar wart on her foot, and I tried the remedy again during a full moon. It worked!

- *Southern Peas (Purple Hull and Cream Peas):* What a wonderful day it was when my husband wanted to grow something in our newly made in-the-ground garden. He had bought the tractor, the tiller attachment, and a row puller for this very reason. I think he really just wanted to buy the tractor but felt he needed to say it was for a garden in order to get me on board. I am so thankful we have the tractor. It makes life so much easier. The garden was formed in June. What in the world were we supposed to plant in the heat of June? Southern peas, which include Purple Hull, Creamed, and Zipper, is what we planted. They grew in a brand new garden that had been amended only with sand, Microlife 6-2-4 fertilizer, and store-bought compost (our compost pile was just beginning). This crop was so easy and productive, I was nothing but amazed. It took a while for them to be ready for harvest. The best indication is when the vein on the outer shell of the pea is deep purple. Harvest and eat them fresh like you would black beans, and store them by blanching and freezing. Cook them the same way as black beans but they will need less time to simmer. They're so easy and so delicious, and they contain high amounts of fiber. They are also a legume that fixes nitrogen into the soil, making the soil ideal for fall planting. The hardest part of them is the shucking. That takes a while but is done easily while watching a romantic comedy or any movie of your choosing.

- *Spinach:* This is such a versatile vegetable, known for feeding the brain exactly what it needs. It contains so many nutrients and can be enjoyed raw or sauteed. Bloomsdale seems to be the best-performing variety. When planting the seeds, it is pertinent to scarify them first. That can be done by using a jar with a light grain sandpaper wrapped around the inside and the smooth side facing the outside of the jar. Place seeds inside the jar, seal it with a lid, and shake the jar in a circular motion. Roselle hibiscus seeds need this kind of attention to germinate as well. Spinach grown by seed tests your patience, and if the soil is too warm, they will not germinate. However, for the impatient gardener, transplants also work well.

Spinach Salad

- Freshly picked, rinsed, and dried spinach
- Homemade croutons (refer to recipe on page 81)
- 3/4 pound freshly fried bacon pieces (reserve 2 tablespoons of bacon grease for the dressing)
- 8 peeled and sliced hard-boiled eggs

Homemade Dressing

- 1/3 cup ketchup
- 1/3 cup red wine vinegar
- 1/3 cup first cold-pressed olive oil
- 2 tablespoons bacon grease
- 3 tablespoons brown sugar

Mix all ingredients together and use immediately; best served warm.

Place spinach in a bowl, add dressing, and mix with hands. Dish out in personal bowls. Add bacon, eggs, and croutons, and serve.

Watch everyone's face in pure ecstasy as they devour the delightful salad.

- *Squash (Yellow, Zucchini, Butternut):* I typically plant all varieties by seed when all the brassicas are finished producing. The yellow summer squash are usually most affected by squash vine borer. The mother (a black moth with a red body looking closely related to a wasp) lays her eggs in the soil, and as they hatch, the borer eats open the vine. An excellent way to prevent this is by making a paste from DE and rubbing it all over the base of the vine, or let nature take its course, which is the approach I take. Squash need to be watered later in the day after their blooms have closed. Getting water in the blooms and a lack of calcium creates blossom end rot. Blanching and freezing is the best way to store excess crops.
- *Strawberries:* Chandler is my go-to strawberry for this climate. It's large, sweet, and performs well in the heat and humidity. I've typically planted them in February when they are available at garden centers; however, I would love to have them available in the fall around October. I think this would give them ample time to get their roots established so by March the plants are huge and produce a lot of fruit. When planted in January or February the plants look awesome and just begin producing right before it becomes too hot and nasty for them. But nonetheless, I plant strawberries every year because they are amazing. I struggled with

them in my raised beds because the roly-poly or pill bug always got to them first. I've used empty cans of wet cat food filled with beer to trap and drown the bugs but have found diatomaceous earth works the best. I've grown them in containers, but the heat gets too intense for their roots, and they quit producing right after they begin. The best place I have found to grow strawberries is in the in-ground garden. It extends the season long enough to get a good production.

- *Sugar Snaps:* These are the sweet gift given in early spring. They are a delight to eat as a snack, fresh or added to stir fries. Whenever my kids say, "Mom I'm hungry," which is their favorite saying, I say, "Go into the garden." Sugar snaps are by far their favorite things to harvest aside from blackberries and strawberries.
- *Tomatoes:* There is nothing more delightful than a vine-ripened tomato. They are completely versatile in so many different dishes or straight from the garden. I have never grown a beautiful tomato plant, but I have always had tomatoes. People who are good at tomatoes are excellent at tomatoes. I'm just okay with growing them. The plants I grow are either beautiful with fruit that gets blossom end rot, or the plants are ugly with beautiful fruit. They are the kid who can't get enough attention.

They need to be staked, need extra shade, and need to be examined daily for leaf-footed stink bugs and their nymphs, as well as hornworms and armyworms. They get blight, get attacked by birds and fruit gets blossom end rot. But the tomato plant made me brave. If you don't have the guts to grab an insect with your hand and smoosh it, kill it, or feed it to the chickens (only the caterpillars), tomatoes will change that about you. Tomatoes love rich, well-draining soil with a lot of fertilizer. If you are using homemade compost with plenty of calcium you will need to add it a few times during the growing season without any additional fertilizer. One year I grew one plant in a large 15-gallon pot using only Strawberry Fields soil from Fox Farm. Hurricane Harvey hit, and we had a record amount of flooding, but my tomatoes were excellent. It got too cold before they were done, but oh how lovely the plant and fruits looked. Freezing or canning fresh tomatoes allows for the harvest to last a very long time.

- *Blossom End Rot:* Tomatoes love water, but too much water without calcium will produce a fruit with blossom end rot. That is why using smashed eggshells in compost is an excellent idea. If you don't have compost, Fox Farm tomato and vegetable fertilizer is wonderful. Just use 1/4 cup per plant. Placing banana peals around the roots adds potassium, and comfrey leaves around the base add extra fertilizer. It's best to plant them in an area where legumes were planted earlier.

- *Staking Tomatoes:* It is important to keep the fruit up off the ground. Indeterminate tomatoes enjoy growing wild and will vine up a trellis. Determinate tomatoes need to be staked by hand or with a heavy-duty tomato cage. This will increase the vigor of the plant and help prevent diseases or insects from eating the fruit.
- *Leaf-Footed Stink Bugs:* These will destroy an entire crop overnight. Their nymphs look like nymphs from the beneficial assassin bugs. As nymphs to adults, the leaf-footed stink bug will use its pointed mouth to pierce through the skin of the fruit to suck out its juices. Piercing the fruit forces the fruit to mature before it's ready. Tomatoes mature from the inside out and when pierced they never have a chance to ripen. When the leaf-footed stink bug is in the nymph stage, they are easiest to kill. Either shake the affected area over a bucket of Dawn dish soap water or squish them with your hand. As they become adults, they are very difficult to kill because of their exoskeleton and flying abilities. I find that capturing them with my hand, throwing them to the ground, and then squashing them with my feet is the best way to

control them. Using a trap crop, such as artichoke, attracts the stink bugs away from the tomatoes.

- *Hornworms:* These are really quite a magnificent caterpillar. They blend in perfectly with the color of tomato plants and will eat a whole plant in the middle of the night. Hornworms are caterpillars of a large moth. In the evening or early morning, they chew the foliage, stems, and fruit of the tomato plant. This is the best time to search for them. In the quiet of the garden if you get really close you can hear them chewing. Remove the caterpillar from the plant and feed it to the chickens.
- *Birds:* Mockingbirds are a threat to tomatoes. You can't kill them as they are the state bird of Texas. Birds only eat the fruit when we are in drought conditions and there is no water. Providing fresh water in a bird bath near the garden is an excellent way to keep them away from the fruit. They will still eat the bugs, and they prefer the protein over the fruit. Having both a bird bath and a fountain will ensure safe fruits.
- *Blight:* This is a virus that will kill the whole plant if it gets out of control. Blight appears on the leaf with a dark spot surrounded by a yellow halo. When the weather is hot and humid in the day and cool (70 degrees and under) in the night, blight is at full force. Helping prevent it by using compost

tea in the spring and/or fall helps build the immunity to blight by forming a protective layer covering the foliage and preventing the virus from penetrating. Also, using compost as mulch works as a protective layer between the soil and foliage of the tomatoes, preventing soil-borne spores from reaching the plant.

- *Turnips:* Chinese turnips are fabulous to grow, producing a smaller more delicate-flavored bulb. The greens produced by turnips are also edible. Turnips help prevent chronic diseases because of their high fiber, high vitamin C, high glucosinolates (helping protect cells from disease-causing damage), and anti-inflammatory and antioxidant properties. Use the fresh greens in salads or stir fries, or roast the bulb with olive oil and salt and pepper. The tender delicate flavor is worth the short period of time it takes to grow them.
- *Watermelon:* This is my second year of growing watermelons, and next year I just know I will have an excellent harvest. Black Diamond are the sworn by variety for our area. I enjoy planting a few seeds in my in-ground garden. I'll plant these in the spring and begin enjoying the fruits of my labor in summer, just in time when our bodies need extra potassium and magnesium from sweating so much. Watermelon has high levels of

these two elements. The trickiest part of growing a delicious watermelon is having enough space and producing delicious fruit. For fruits and vegetables to have excellent flavor, the appropriate trace minerals need to be present in the soil. Azomite, which is harvested from the volcanic ash in the seabed, contains every trace mineral and element. It only needs to be applied once every three to five years or when needed. If your garden is a mature 3-year-old with plenty of compost you will not have an issue of flavor. Watermelon fruit needs to be shaded, but the vines need full sun. If the fruit remains exposed to full sun, it will cause a sunburn. The fruit is ready to be harvested when the stem releases with no effort. Let it sit outside for a few days, inside for a few days, and then in the refrigerator for a few days before eating. The watermelons we don't eat are an exceptional treat to our chickens when heat is zapping them of necessary nutrients and water. After feeding the chickens their watermelon treat, they are so sweet and healthy looking like they just received a refreshing day at the spa.

The Power of the Rose

The most used and admired plant in our garden is the rose. In spring and fall, when the weather is cooler, the fragrance from the roses fills the air. That fragrance has physiological and psychological effects such as relaxation and anti-anxiety. Applying rose water to the skin is healing as well. It works to help reduce inflammation, whiten skin, smooth wrinkles, heal sunburns, and relieve skin irritations from poison ivy, sunburns, mosquito bites, and ant bites.

I was twelve when I had my first experience with rose water. Twelve was a formative age for me. My parents were going through a divorce, and it seemed as though they cared about nobody but themselves, which as an adult I now understand. The stress of divorce is so powerful. Adults are just trying to keep breathing. Stress oozed all over our family. My sister was gone at college, drinking away her stress. My dad did yoga, worked out, worked all the time, and was dating other women to relieve his stress. My mom survived on coffee, ice cream, and popcorn and dated other men to cope with the stress. I was left feeling completely alone.

I cried every day when I was twelve and thirteen. So when a friend asked me to stay the night at her house, hope for some normalcy filled my heart.

In my memory, her house was white with hardwood floors. There were many windows that allowed the natural light to flow through every room. Her room was lovingly messy with art everywhere, fabric of different colors and textures, beads, feathers, and a dream space for creative minds. The kitchen had tall ceilings and tall white cupboards, some with glass as doors and some with solid wood painted white. There was a tile island in the middle of the kitchen where we sat and chatted with her mom who made us a dinner I can't recall, but I remember everything about the dessert. Her mother asked if I had ever had rose ice cream. She said it was a favorite dessert from her Jewish culture. In two bowls, one for her daughter and one for me, she scooped plain vanilla ice cream. Reaching into the cabinet, my friend's mom pulled out a clear bottle of rose water and added a few drops to our ice cream. The flavor, smell, and feeling that arose inside of me is still fresh in my mind like it was just yesterday. I was weary of trying new things, and I was still a child, so my first bite was itsy bitsy. But the impact was huge—cold sugary milk with a hint of rose that seemed stronger as I exhaled through my nose. It was the fanciest thing I had ever tasted, and it made me feel sophisticated and elegant. I remember nothing else from that sleepover except the feeling of being loved and cared for because of rose ice cream.

Throughout the following thirty plus years, I have tried unsuccessfully to recreate the rose ice cream. Regular rose water does not work. I have bought several food-grade rose waters online, and they do not meet my expectations. Distilling my home-grown roses would be the most likely solution, but I have not yet begun that hobby.

In 2020 when everything was shut down, I ran out of a really expensive facial moisturizer I had been using. Spending so much time at home with my two girls, I began researching homemade facial moisturizer for oily skin. There was a recipe I really liked that used fresh aloe vera flesh, rose water, and vitamin C powder, all blended in a food processor. Using vitamin E in the concoction helped keep it from spoiling too quickly. But then I became lazy and only wanted to do one step of the process—making the rose water and using just that as a toner. When I gave the toner and the aloe gel moisturizer to a friend of mine with really inflamed facial skin, she swore up and down it was the rose water that took the inflammation away, evening out her skin tone and soothing her face. She began planning her first garden in the first house she ever owned and said the only plants she would have were Texas natives and roses so she could garden with little effort and make her own rose water for her face.

Rose water for my face is all I need. It moisturizes, reduces fine lines, lightens age spots, evens skin tones, and protects against sun damage and harmful toxins in the air. I take rose water with me wherever I go, even on camping trips with the

Girl Scouts, which is where I learned of its other benefits. We had a girl get into poison ivy, and after applying calamine lotion, she was still itchy. Just for fun I sprayed some rose water on her itching skin, and immediately the irritation went away. On that same trip, another girl who gets sunburned just looking outside came back from the beach with burned red skin. I sprayed her with rose water, and she too was instantly relieved, not needing anything else.

There is a trick to making healing rose water. Growing your own roses is the start. Roses we buy from stores are all heavily treated with chemicals. Growers have to treat roses heavily with insecticides and fungicides. It's not that growers want to be dependent on synthetic chemicals, but most are for now. One grower here in Houston is making the switch to 90 percent organic and 10 percent synthetic practices. Developing new varieties with strong disease resistance is also helping reduce the need for fungicides. It's not a fast process, but being in the horticulture industry, I'm seeing a shift to a more sustainable approach to growing by implementing technology, breeding for stronger and more resilient genetics, implementing beneficial microbes, and adding the right minerals and nutrients into our growing practices. But we are not quite there yet, and like humans, sometimes we do need to implement something stronger than natural to combat illnesses 10 percent of the time.

It takes one year of growth after planting roses for them to be organic. I've noticed that applying compost tea for the first year or two, only twice a year, once in the fall and once in the spring—builds the immune system enough to naturally fight off diseases and viruses. Lighter colored flowers (light pink and white) are susceptible to thrips that get in the buds and suck out all the juices, turning the buds brown and dying off before ever opening. Thrips are most prevalent in spring but cannot withstand the heat of summer. Most roses will bloom the majority of the year, except in cold winters. Hybrid tea roses are the typical rose used for fresh-cut arrangements, while floribunda typically produce clusters of more delicate lacy blooms. Shrub roses are grown for use as a shrub in the landscape and produce several small blooms throughout the year. All roses work for making tea. On Valentine's Day, roses benefit from a good heavy prune, which is a good time to fertilize using organic fertilizers, compost, or compost tea only.

When new growth begins to appear (recognizable by the reddish foliage), pinch them back a couple inches. Doing that allows the plant to become bushier and produce more blooms. Harvesting is best done in the morning after the morning dew has dried, cutting the bloom from the stem at the base of the flower. The oil content in the rose is at its highest levels at this time.

Rose Water

Using distilled or reverse osmosis water, bring a half cup water to a boil in a stainless steel, covered, small saucepan.

Add fresh or dried roses and two dried calendula flowers, stirring with a metal spoon until all flowers are just barely covered in water.

Cover, turn heat off, and let cool on the stovetop until it's room temperature.

Strain the cooled rose water into a liquid measuring cup.

Fill a glass spray bottle. Store any extra in a glass jar with a plastic lid.

Store all tea in the refrigerator. It will last six or more weeks.

Use whenever and however you so desire. I use it religiously in the morning and night after washing my face.

The Goal of Gardening

In the beginning, my goal of gardening was to host fabulous dinner parties with my friends using homegrown herbs, adding a little touch of health to our otherwise booze-filled evening with dancing, laughter, conversation, and bonding.

Then the goal was to create a little comfortable home with my then-live-in boyfriend. It was to add beauty and life to our neighborhood and have fresh-cut flowers at our table when we ate.

Later, the goal was to have healthy children who could crawl all around our yard and put in their mouths whatever they were curious about and wanted to explore. It was to feed the healthiest and most nutritious food to them without adding manmade supplements. Essentially, it was to give our children a healthy start in life. The dinner table is where we bond every day. The kitchen is where I bonded with my mom, drinking, baking, and cooking Thanksgiving dinners. And now it's where I bond with my stepmom, my mother in law, my sister, my girls, my husband, and my friends.

I know the amount of energy and love I put into growing

all plants and cooking food. It is my way of showing the ones I love just how much I love them. I love them so much that I will do anything in my power to make sure they get the purest and most wholesome food that nourishes their mind, body, and soul.

The goal of gardening is letting go of control and practicing patience, grace, and forgiveness. It is about watching the miracle of life unfold before your very eyes. It's letting nature take control and work out its own problems but giving consistent support so it can thrive.

The goal is to make connections with the earth and sky, to connect to family, to connect with friends and strangers, to share love and hope instead of fear.

The goal is to know that one life has breathed more easily because I have lived. It is to provide independence from the government and society by producing our own food that is completely chemical-free and in abundant supply even when the grocery store runs out. It's about creating a space that draws in all life—birds, bees, random animals, and people. And the goal of gardening is to be closer to God and more in touch with what is real and important in life.

Epilogue

Writing this book has been intertwined with a very big health issue I discovered I had soon after I began writing. After I had COVID in September 2020, I struggled to regain energy and was increasingly becoming more susceptible to getting sick. A year later, I knew something had to change. I needed to get to the root cause of what was happening to me. COVID changed the way I thought and how much I blindly trusted doctors. I found a doctor—my current gynecologist—whom I completely trust. And she encouraged me to do my own research and trust my instincts. I asked her to check everything about me—everything in my blood, my hormones, estrogen levels, vitamin D levels, HIV, and hepatitis C. My mother was a drug user and a product of the 1960s. It turns out that I had hepatitis C and have had it my entire life. I lived until the ripe age of forty-two without any issues—even when treating my body poorly, drinking, smoking, doing drugs, working in the horticultural industry which is so highly dependent on chemicals, and floating in rivers downstream from large industrial growers.

My liver was damaged and it was telling me. It told me in yoga when I would do certain movements, and it would cramp up and be almost unbearable. When I drank more than three glasses of wine, it took me one full week to feel good again. My poop was a light brown to yellow at times. My nails were brittle, and my hair was thinning out. I had zero energy and dark circles under my eyes. I bruised easily, spider veins spread on my legs, my emotions were not stable, I was tired beyond belief, nightmares were a normal occurrence, I could not build up muscle, I had a cognitive problem making sense of words or ideas, and my recollection was horrible. I have had several of these issues most if not all my life, which has made it hard for me to determine what was a normal, healthy sign. Luckily, we caught it when we did. When the ultrasound was completed, the scar tissue on my liver was not quite at the cirrhosis level, but it was almost there. I was at the verge of liver failure if I didn't kill the virus. So that's what I did—three months of pills and no alcohol.

I need to add here that I was a big drinker and smoker and occasional pot smoker from college until my first pregnancy. I quit smoking and drinking before I got pregnant with my first child and only drank on rare occasions for her first fourteen months of life because that's how long I breastfed. It was the same with my second child. Having kids saved my life. It really pushed me to do the very best for the future of my children, in turn giving me a reason to eat healthily and be active in the outdoors on a daily basis. Prior to children, I truly did not care about myself. I didn't hate myself; I just never loved myself enough to care if I was healthy or not.

My virus: It was mine. We were born together, grew up together, and lived with each other my entire life. It was older than I was. It was part of my mother before it was part of me. It was my last connection to my mom that she couldn't take away from me. That virus—my virus—was freed of my body in 2023. I expected to feel a giant change, but everything was the same. My liver was still sick, my allergies were out of control, I couldn't take certain allergy medications because they gave me nightmares of killing my kids, and I was desperate to find a way to cure my allergies to pollen naturally. Remembering my first pregnancy and how horrible my allergies were because of hormone changes, I decided to find what part of my body was in control of my hormones and take care of that part. It was my liver. The liver is in control of hormones. It is in charge of hundreds of jobs, including regulating blood chemical levels, converting toxins to waste, purifying the blood, helping with digestion, removing red blood cells, and helping regulate hormones. Long story short, I did a ten-day liver cleanse and finally started to feel better.

Naturally healing the liver is the same thing you would do for any autoimmune disease, mental health issue, building a fat fluffy brain, or increasing your immune system.

Some exercise, eating a Mediterranean diet (high in healthy fats, low in sugar and seed oils), and getting eight hours of sleep. It's not profound, and it doesn't have to happen overnight. It can be done by making little changes and eventually developing habits. Taking a digestion walk (20–30 minute fast-paced walk) after dinner gets the blood flowing all over the body, improving digestion and assisting in a full night's sleep. Making food from scratch using the right fats such as olive oil (first cold-pressed); frying in lard, tallow, coconut oil, or ghee; or eating grass-fed butter allows for healthier choices. Cut back on sugar by making desserts from scratch. Staying busy during the day, going to bed at the same time each night, and waking up early allows for an excellent night's sleep. Investing in high-quality bedding also helps to get a peaceful nights rest.

Over a year has passed since my ten-day liver cleanse and making minor adjustments to my lifestyle. I've had another ultrasound, and my liver is healing. While it's not fully healed, I feel better than I ever have. A fully healed liver could take up to three years, just like soil, just like polluted waters, just like the ocean. We are all capable of healing; we just need to make minor adjustments here and there, and eventually the practices become easy. Stop using as many chemicals in gardens, agriculture, horticulture, or water. If we are gentle with ourselves, we allow ourselves an opportunity to filter out toxins naturally and can rebuild healthy cells and lipids that protect our cells. And it doesn't take much.

I understand all too well about wanting to perfect everything, including diet and health, but that perfection only pushes me away from making even the smallest changes that work. If I feel good and healthy, I'm doing good. When I feel bad and sluggish, I need to change something. When I feel good, I am sweet, kind, and loving to all humans and all living things. Imagine what this world would be like if everyone felt good.

www.ingramcontent.com/pod-product-compliance
Lightning Source LLC
LaVergne TN
LVHW010609100826
845148LV00014B/2900

* 9 7 8 1 6 8 4 8 8 1 5 2 9 *